The Wild Muir

The Wild Muir

Twenty-two of John Muir's Greatest Adventures

Selected and Introduced by
LEE STETSON

Illustrated by
FIONA KING

YOSEMITE ASSOCIATION
Yosemite National Park, California

Yosemite Association
P. O. Box 545
Yosemite National Park, California 95389

The Yosemite Association
is a non-profit, membership organization
dedicated to the support of Yosemite National Park.
Our publishing program is designed to provide
an educational service and to increase the public's
understanding of Yosemite's special qualities and needs.
To learn more about our activities and other publications,
or for information about membership, please write to
the address above, or call (209) 379-2646.

Library of Congress Cataloging-in-Publication Data
Muir, John, 1838–1914.
The wild Muir: twenty-two of John Muir's greatest adventures /
selected and introduced by Lee Stetson; illustrated by Fiona King.
p. cm.
ISBN 0-939666-75-8
1. Muir, John, 1838–1914. 2. Naturalists—United States—
Biography. I. Stetson, Lee. II. Yosemite Association.
III. Title.
QH31.M78A3 1994
333.72' 2' 092—dc20
[B] 94-20052
CIP

For the many thousands who have enjoyed
the reincarnated Muir
in Yosemite and elsewhere,
and most especially
for my loving and
much loved
Connie.

Contents

Introduction

For all his lofty thoughts, for all his contributions and discoveries, I suspect that John Muir would long ago have faded into relative obscurity, save for his amazing adventures. Muir engaged wildness with perhaps more enthusiastic love and passionate courage than any other American before or after him. Usually alone, with little more than bread and tea for sustenance, often without coat or blanket, Muir eagerly explored the mountains of the American West. His written accounts of the events that befell him during his travels are astounding, amazing and almost unbelievable.

In fact, as an actor who regularly dramatizes many of these adventures, I am most often asked, "Do you think Muir *really* did that?" Well, I do. So did his contemporaries; no one who knew him or traveled with him doubted his word. Questioning Muir's veracity is commonplace enough nowadays—the strength and stamina required to undertake these adventures suggest to many exaggeration, and to some, outright fabrication. My years of research suggest, however, that Muir was not only truthful in his writing, but in some instances quite modest.

Given the sheer quantity of Muir's work, remarkably little of it involves personal narrative. Much is descriptive commentary common to travelogues of the day (though generally of much better quality), some is scientific study and opinion, and a good deal is general sermonizing about the healthful effect of engaging wildness. Muir was often hounded by editors and friends to write more of his adventures and less of everything else, but he was reluctant to do so, confiding in his journals that he preferred to be a sort of prism, "a flake of glass through which the light passes."

Except for the "scootchers" of his childhood (the games of daring that he and the other children enjoyed), Muir never seemed to seek adventure for adventure's sake. His rationale was constant—curiosity and study were what motivated him, and wonder, exhilaration and learning were the rewards. Examples abound. He confronted and *charged* a large bear, hoping to make it bolt so that he could "study his gait in running;" "eager to see as many avalanches as possible," he was caught up in one; tossed violently about the Yosemite Valley floor during California's biggest earthquake, he was sure he was "going to learn something;" and "anxious to learn more of this curious hill," he climbed a 500-foot wall of ice beneath the great Yosemite Fall.

The risks were real, but measured with the eye of a true mountaineer. "Accidents in the mountains," he wrote, "are less common than in the lowlands, and these mountain mansions are decent, delightful, even divine, places to die in, compared with the doleful chambers of civilization. Few places in this world are more dangerous than home. Fear not, therefore, to try the mountain-passes. They will kill care, save you from deadly apathy, set you free, and call forth every faculty into vigorous, enthusiastic action."

The Wild Muir was conceived as a book offering only wilderness adventures in which Muir's life or limb was threatened. When the final selections had been made, however, not all of the stories satisfied the original criteria. A purist, knowing of Muir's rugged constitution and his skill and ease in the out-of-doors, might consider it misleading to include the famous tree ride. His feelings were certainly those of sheer delight, not fear or threat. And three of these episodes—his brush with death at the bottom of the well, the industrial accident that nearly blinded him in Indianapolis, and the fever encountered in Florida—would be more properly labelled *mis*-adventures.

In all, twenty-two extraordinary, death-defying stories are included here. Written in his own words, they begin in childhood and continue chronologically through Muir's fifty-second year. The accounts all share Muir's zest for living and for everything that he encountered, and reflect some of his best and most engaging writing. The Victorian flourish and sense of leisure common to much of his prose are notably absent from this collection.

Besides Muir's writings, two other accounts supporting and amplifying Muir's versions of events are included in this volume. The first, part of a government report describing Muir's return from the violent storm on Mount Shasta, has never before been published (to the best of my knowledge). It provides several details of his suffering that Muir either neglected to mention or found unimportant. The other, S. Hall Young's wonderful account of the rescue on Glenora Peak, gives us a sharply observed view of Muir as the vigorous mountaineer. It comes from Young's *Alaska Days with John Muir*, and makes a fine counterpoint to Muir's version of the same episode.

The real purpose of *The Wild Muir*, however, is not to provide biography, to answer or raise questions, to fill in historical gaps, or to add to the endless conjecture about the true character of John Muir (though it does all of these things to some degree). It is simply to provide the reader a rousing good time. Twenty-two rousing good times. May you enjoy the adventure!

Lee Stetson
El Portal, California

The Adventures

Good Scootchers

Born in Scotland on April 21, 1838, John Muir made early excursions into life- and limb-endangering activities that were undoubtedly typical of any high-spirited boy in the small town of Dunbar, on the North Sea. Muir called these games of daring "scootchers." From The Story of My Boyhood and Youth *comes this account of the future mountaineer's first ascents, and of his first rescue of a fellow adventurer.*

While Muir is still relatively unknown in Scotland, the East Lothian District Council in Dunbar has honored its native son; his early seashore playground has been preserved as the John Muir Country Park, and the attic of the Muir home has been set aside as a museum. Even more appropriately, in 1984 the John Muir Trust was established to acquire wild lands in Britain.

When I was a boy in Scotland I was fond of everything that was wild, and all my life I've been growing fonder and fonder of wild places and wild creatures. Fortunately around my native town of Dunbar, by the stormy North Sea, there was no lack of wildness, though most of the land lay in smooth cultivation. With red-blooded playmates, wild as myself, I loved to wander in the fields to hear the birds sing, and along the seashore to gaze and wonder at the shells and seaweeds, eels and crabs in the pools among the rocks when the tide was low; and best of all to watch the waves in awful storms thundering on the black headlands and craggy ruins of the old Dunbar Castle when the sea and the sky, the waves and the clouds, were mingled together as one.

* * *

One of our best playgrounds was the famous old Dunbar Castle, to which King Edward fled after his defeat at Bannockburn. It was built more than a thousand years ago, and though we knew little of its history, we had heard many mysterious stories of the battles fought about its walls, and firmly believed that every bone we found in the ruins belonged to an ancient warrior. We tried to see who could climb highest on the crumbling peaks and crags, and took chances that no cautious mountaineer would try. That I did not fall and finish my rock-scrambling in those adventurous boyhood days seems now a reasonable wonder.

Among our best games were running, jumping, wrestling, and scrambling. I was so proud of my skill as a climber that when I first heard of hell from a servant girl who loved to tell its horrors and warn us that if we did anything wrong we would be cast into it, I always insisted that I could climb out of it. I imagined it was only a sooty pit with stone walls like those of the castle, and I felt sure there must be chunks and cracks in the masonry for fingers and toes. Anyhow the terrors of the horrible place seldom lasted long beyond the telling; for natural faith casts out fear.

Most of the Scotch children believe in ghosts, and some under peculiar conditions continue to believe in them all through life. Grave ghosts are deemed particularly dangerous, and many of the most credulous will go far out of their way to avoid passing through or near a graveyard in the dark. After being instructed by the servants in the nature, looks, and habits of the various black and white ghosts, boowuzzies, and witches we often speculated as to whether they could run fast, and tried to believe that we had a good chance to get away from most of them. To improve our speed and wind, we often took long runs into the country. Tam o'Shanter's mare outran a lot of witches,—at least until she reached a place of safety beyond the keystone of the bridge,—and we thought perhaps we also might be able to outrun them.

Our house formerly belonged to a physician, and a servant girl told us that the ghost of the dead doctor haunted one of the unoccupied rooms in the second story that was kept dark on account of a heavy window-tax. Our bedroom was adjacent to the ghost room, which had in it a lot of chemical apparatus,—glass tubing, glass and brass retorts, test-tubes, flasks, etc.,—and we thought that those strange articles were still used by the old dead doctor in compounding physic. In the long summer days David and I were put to bed several hours before sunset. Mother tucked us in carefully, drew the curtains of the big old-fashioned bed, and told us to lie still and sleep like gude bairns; but we were usually out of bed, playing games of daring called "scootchers," about as soon as our loving mother reached the foot of the stairs, for we couldn't lie still, however hard we might try. Going into the ghost room was regarded as a very great scootcher. After venturing in a few steps and rushing back in terror, I used to dare David to go as far without getting caught.

The roof of our house, as well as the crags and walls of the old castle, offered fine mountaineering exercise. Our bedroom was lighted by a dormer window. One night I opened it in search of good scootchers and hung myself out over the slates, holding on to the sill, while the wind was making a balloon of my nightgown. I then dared David to try the adventure, and he did. Then I went out again and hung by one hand, and David did the same. Then I hung by one finger, being careful not to slip, and he did that too. Then I stood on the sill and examined the edge of the left wall of the window, crept up the slates along its side by slight finger-holds, got astride of the roof, sat there a few minutes looking at the scenery over the garden wall while the wind was howling and threatening to blow me off, then managed to slip down, catch hold of the sill, and get safely back into the room. But before attempting this scootcher, recognizing its dangerous character, with commendable caution I warned David that in case I should happen to slip I would grip the rain-trough when I was going over the eaves and hang on, and that he must then run fast downstairs and tell father to get a ladder for me, and tell him to be quick because I would soon be tired hanging dangling in the wind by my hands. After my return from this capital scootcher, David, not to be outdone, crawled up to the top of the window-roof, and got bravely astride of it; but in trying to return he lost courage and began to greet (to cry), "I canna get doon. Oh, I canna get doon." I leaned out of the window and shouted encouragingly, "Dinna greet, Davie, dinna greet, I'll help ye doon. If you greet, fayther will hear, and gee us baith an awfu' skelping." Then, standing on the sill and holding on by one hand to the window-casing, I directed him to slip his feet down within reach, and, after securing a good hold, I jumped inside and dragged him in by his heels. This finished scootcher-scrambling for the night and frightened us into bed.

Excerpted from *The Story of My Boyhood and Youth*. Boston and New York: Houghton Mifflin Company, 1913.

Near Drowning

In 1849, Daniel Muir, John's tyrannical father, took his family to the wilderness of Wisconsin to homestead an idyllic 80 acres known as Fountain Lake. A religious extremist, Daniel worked his eight sons and daughters seventeen hours a day to produce wheat and corn, the sale of which provided support to distant missions. This relentless regime of work was relieved only on Sunday afternoons, on the first of January, and on the Fourth of July, for "all the others were labor-days, rain or shine, cold or warm."

The idea of recreation was generally alien to hard-working Scottish immigrants, but the homestead's lake provided an irresistible "old swimming hole" for the young Muir, and this memorable Fourth of July incident allows us insight into his developing character.

ONE HOT SUMMER DAY father told us that we ought to learn to swim. This was one of the most interesting suggestions he had ever offered, but precious little time was allowed for trips to the lake, and he seldom tried to show us how. "Go to the frogs," he said, "and they will give you all the lessons you need. Watch their arms and legs and see how smoothly they kick themselves along and dive and come up. When you want to dive, keep your arms by your side or over your head, and kick, and when you want to come up, let your legs drag and paddle with your hands."

We found a little basin among the rushes at the south end of the lake, about waist-deep and a rod or two wide, shaped like a sunfish's nest. Here we kicked and plashed for many a lesson, faithfully trying to imitate frogs; but the smooth, comfortable sliding gait of our amphibious teachers seemed hopelessly hard to learn. When we tried to kick frog-fashion, down went our heads as if weighted with lead the moment our feet left the ground. One day it occurred to me to hold my breath as long as I could and let my head sink as far as it liked without paying any attention to it, and try to swim under the water instead of on the surface. This method was a great success, for at the very first trial I managed to cross the basin without touching bottom, and soon learned the use of my limbs. Then, of course, swimming with my head above water soon became so easy that it seemed perfectly natural. David tried the plan with the same success. Then we began to count the number of times that we could swim around the basin without stopping to rest, and after twenty or thirty rounds failed to tire us, we proudly thought that a little more practice would make us about as amphibious as frogs.

On the fourth of July of the swimming year one of the Lawson boys came to visit us, and we went down to the lake to spend the great warm day with the fishes and ducks and turtles. After gliding about on the smooth mirror water, telling stories and enjoying the company of the happy creatures about us, we rowed to our bathing-pool, and David and I went in for a swim, while our companion fished from the boat a little way out beyond the rushes. After a few turns in the pool, it occurred to me that it was now about time to try deep water. Swimming through the thick growth of rushes and lilies was somewhat dangerous, especially for a beginner, because one's arms and legs might be entangled among the long, limber stems; nevertheless I ventured and struck out boldly enough for the boat, where the water was twenty or thirty feet deep. When I reached the end of the little skiff I raised my right hand to take hold of it to surprise Lawson, whose back was toward me and who was not aware of my approach; but I failed to reach high enough, and, of course, the weight of my arm and the stroke against the overleaning stern of the boat shoved me down and I sank, struggling, frightened and confused. As soon as my feet touched the bottom, I slowly rose to the surface, but before I could get breath enough to call for help, sank back again and lost all control of myself. After sinking and rising I don't know how many times, some water got into my lungs and I began to drown. Then suddenly my mind seemed to clear. I remembered that I could swim under water, and, making a desperate struggle toward the shore, I reached a point where with my toes on the bottom I got my mouth above the surface, gasped for help, and was pulled into the boat.

This humiliating accident spoiled the day, and we all agreed to keep it a profound secret. My sister Sarah had heard my cry for help, and on our arrival at the house inquired what had happened. "Were you drowning, John? I heard you cry you couldna get oot." Lawson made haste to reply, "Oh, no! He was juist haverin" [making fun].

I was very much ashamed of myself, and at night, after calmly reviewing the affair, concluded that there had been no reasonable cause for the accident, and that I ought to punish myself for so nearly losing my life from unmanly fear. Accordingly at the very first opportunity, I stole away to the lake by myself, got into my boat, and instead of going back to the old swimming-bowl for further practice, or to try to do sanely and well what I had so ignominiously failed to do in my first adventure, that is, to swim out through the rushes and lilies, I rowed directly out to the middle of the lake, stripped, stood up on the seat in the stern, and with grim deliberation took a header and dove straight down thirty or forty feet, turned easily, and, letting my feet drag, paddled straight to the surface with my hands as father had at first directed me to do. I then swam round the boat, glorying in my suddenly acquired confidence and victory over myself, climbed into it, and dived again, with the same triumphant success. I think I went down four or five times, and each time as I made the dive-spring shouted aloud, "Take that!" feeling that I was getting most gloriously even with myself.

Never again from that day to this have I lost control of myself in water. If suddenly thrown overboard at sea in the dark, or even while asleep, I think I would immediately right myself in a way some would call "instinct," rise among the waves, catch my breath, and try to plan what would better be done. Never was victory over self more complete. I have been a good swimmer ever since. At a slow gait I think I could swim all day in smooth water moderate in temperature. When I was a student at Madison, I used to go on long swimming-journeys, called exploring expeditions, along the south shore of Lake Mendota, on Saturdays, sometimes alone, sometimes with another amphibious explorer by the name of Fuller.

My adventures in Fountain Lake call to mind the story of a boy who in climbing a tree to rob a crow's nest fell and broke his leg, but as soon as it healed compelled himself to climb to the top of the tree he had fallen from.

Like Scotch children in general we were taught grim self-denial, in season and out of season, to mortify the flesh, keep our bodies in subjection to Bible laws, and mercilessly punish ourselves for every fault imagined or committed. A little boy, while helping his sister to drive home the cows, happened to use a forbidden word. "I'll have to tell fayther on ye," said the horrified sister. "I'll tell him that ye said a bad word." "Weel," said the boy, by way of excuse, "I couldna help the word comin' into me, and it's na waur to speak it oot than to let it rin through ye."

A Scotch fiddler playing at a wedding drank so much whiskey that on the way home he fell by the roadside. In the morning he was ashamed and angry and determined to punish himself. Making haste to the house of a friend, a gamekeeper, he called him out, and requested the loan of a gun. The alarmed gamekeeper, not liking the fiddler's looks and voice, anxiously inquired what he was going to do with it. "Surely," said he, "you're no gan to shoot yoursel." "No-o," with characteristic candor replied the penitent fiddler, "I dinna think that I'll juist exactly kill mysel, but I'm gaun to tak a dander doon the burn (brook) wi' the gun and gie mysel a deevil o' a fleg" (fright).

Excerpted from *The Story of My Boyhood and Youth*. Boston and New York: Houghton Mifflin Company, 1913.

At the Bottom of the Well

The poor soil of the Fountain Lake farm prompted Daniel Muir to seek richer pastures in 1857. The nineteen-year-old John and his siblings had been worked into near exhaustion to extract the bounty of the "home eighty," but were to remain "slaves through the vice of over-industry" for a few more years, homesteading another 400 acres, called Hickory Hill Farm. The well described within this story, sunk "straight and plumb," provides water even today.

After eight years of this dreary work of clearing the Fountain Lake farm, fencing it and getting it in perfect order, building a frame house and the necessary outbuildings for the cattle and horses,—after all this had been victoriously accomplished, and we had made out to escape with life,—father bought a half-section of wild land about four or five miles to the eastward and began all over again to clear and fence and break up other fields for a new farm, doubling all the stunting, heart-breaking chopping, grubbing, stump-digging, rail-splitting, fence-building, barn-building, house-building, and so forth.

* * *

We called our second farm Hickory Hill, from its many fine hickory trees and the long gentle slope leading up to it. Compared with Fountain Lake farm it lay high and dry. The land was better, but it had no living water, no spring or stream or meadow or lake. A well ninety feet deep had to be dug, all except the first ten feet or so in fine-grained sandstone. When the sandstone was struck, my father, on the advice of a man who had worked in mines, tried to blast the rock; but from lack of skill the blasting went on very slowly, and father decided to have me do all the work with mason's chisels, a long, hard job, with a good deal of danger in it. I had to sit cramped in a space about three feet in diameter, and wearily chip, chip, with heavy hammer and chisels from early morning until dark, day after day, for weeks and months. In the morning, father and David lowered me in a wooden bucket by a windlass, hauled up what chips were left from the night before, then went away to the farm work and left me until noon, when they hoisted me out for dinner. After dinner I was promptly lowered again, the forenoon's accumulation of chips hoisted out of the way, and I was left until night.

One morning, after the dreary bore was about eighty feet deep, my life was all but lost in deadly choke-damp,—carbonic acid gas that had settled at the bottom during the night. Instead of clearing away the chips as usual when I was lowered to the bottom, I swayed back and forth and began to sink under the poison. Father, alarmed that I did not make any noise, shouted, "What's keeping you so still?" to which he got no reply. Just as I was settling down against the side of the wall, I happened to catch a glimpse of a branch of a bur-oak tree which leaned out over the mouth of the shaft. This suddenly awakened me, and to father's excited shouting I feebly murmured, "Take me out." But when he began to hoist he found I was not in the bucket and in wild alarm shouted, "Get in! Get in the bucket and hold on! Hold on!" Somehow I managed to get into the bucket, and that is all I remembered until I was dragged out, violently gasping for breath.

One of our near neighbors, a stone mason and miner by the name of William Duncan, came to see me, and after hearing the particulars of the accident he solemnly said: "Weel, Johnnie, it's God's mercy that you're alive. Many a companion of mine have I seen dead with choke-damp, but none that I ever saw or heard of was so near to death in it as you were and escaped without help." Mr. Duncan taught father to throw water down the shaft to absorb the gas, and also to drop a bundle of brush or hay attached to a light rope, dropping it again and again to carry down pure air and stir up the poison. When, after a day or two, I had recovered from the shock, father lowered me again to my work, after taking the precaution to test the air with a candle and stir it up well with a brush-and-hay bundle. The weary hammer-and-chisel-chipping went on as before, only more slowly, until ninety feet down, when at last I struck a fine, hearty gush of water. Constant dropping wears away stone. So does constant chipping, while at the same time wearing away the chipper. Father never spent an hour in that well. He trusted me to sink it straight and plumb, and I did, and built a fine covered top over it, and swung two iron-bound buckets in it from which we all drank for many a day.

Excerpted from *The Story of My Boyhood and Youth*. Boston and New York: Houghton Mifflin Company, 1913.

NOTE

Many years later, scribbling in his notebook while wandering in California, Muir had occasion to recall the well story.

Tell me what you will of the benefactions of city civilization, of the sweet security of streets—all as part of the natural upgrowth of man towards the high destiny we hear so much of. I know that our bodies were made to thrive only in pure air, and the scenes in which pure air is found. If the death exhalations that brood the broad towns in which we so fondly compact ourselves were made visible, we should flee as from a plague. All are more or less sick; there is not a perfectly sane man in San Francisco.

Go now and then for fresh life—if most of humanity must go through this town stage of development—just as divers hold their breath and come ever and anon to the surface to breathe. . . Go whether or not you have faith. . . Form parties, if you must be social, to go to the snow-flowers in winter, to sun-flowers in summer. . . Anyway, go up and away for life; be fleet!

I know some will heed the warning. Most will not, so full of pagan slavery is the boasted freedom of the town, and those who need rest and clean snow and sky the most will be the last to move.

Once I was let down into a deep well into which choke-damp had settled, and nearly lost my life. The deeper I was immersed in the invisible poison, the less capable I became of willing measures of escape from it. And in just this Condition are those who toil or dawdle or dissipate in crowded towns, in the sinks of commerce or pleasure.

When I first came down to the city from my mountain home, I began to wither, and wish instinctively for the vital woods and high sky. Yet I lingered month after month, plodding at "duty." At length I chanced to see a lovely goldenrod in bloom in a weedy spot alongside one of the less frequented sidewalks there. Suddenly I was aware of the ending of summer and fled. Then, once away, I saw how shrunken and lean I was, and how glad I was I had gone. . .

Blind!

Extracting precious time from the daily drudgery of farm work, young John Muir spent his pre-dawn hours inventing a variety of machines. After four years of fitful schooling at the University of Wisconsin at Madison, Muir found outlet for his talent through employment, first in Canada, then in Indiana. The accident recounted here occurred in March of 1867. It led directly to Muir's renewed commitment to the wilderness, helping prompt his decision "to devote the rest of my life to the study of the inventions of God."

LOOKING OVER THE MAP I saw that Indianapolis was an important railroad center, and probably had manufactories of different sorts in which I could find employment, with the advantage of being in the heart of one of the very richest forests of deciduous hard wood trees on the continent. Here I was successful in gaining employment in a carriage material factory full of circular saws and chucks and eccentric and concentric lathes, etc. I first worked for ten dollar a week, without board, of course. The second week my wages were increased to eighteen a week, and later to about twenty-five a week. I greatly enjoyed this mechanical work, began to invent and introduce labor-saving improvements and was so successful that my botanical and geological studies were in danger of being seriously interrupted.

One day a member of the firm asked me, "How long are you going to stay with us?" "Not long," I said. "Just long enough to earn a few hundred dollars, then I am going on with my studies in the woods." He said, "You are doing very well, and if you will stop, we will give you the foremanship of the shop," and held out hopes of a partnership interest in the money-making business. To this I replied that although I liked the inventive work and the earnest rush and roar and whirl of the factory, Nature's attractions were stronger and I must soon get away.

A serious accident hurried me away sooner than I had planned. I had put in a countershaft for a new circular saw and as the belt connecting with the main shaft was new it stretched considerably after running a few hours and had to be shortened. While I was unlacing it, making use of the nail-like end of a file to draw out the stitches, it slipped and pierced my right eye on the edge of the cornea. After the first shock was over I closed my eye, and when I lifted the lid of the injured one the aqueous humor dripped on my hand—the sight gradually failed and in a few minutes came perfect darkness. "My right eye is gone," I murmured, "closed forever on all God's beauty." At first I felt no particular weakness. I walked steadily enough to the house where I was boarding, but in a few hours the shock sent me trembling to bed, and very soon by sympathy the other eye became blind, so that I was in total darkness and feared that I would become permanently blind.

When Professor Butler learned that I was in Indianapolis, he sent me a letter of introduction to one of the best families there, and in some way they heard of the accident and came to see me and brought an oculist, who had studied abroad, to examine the pierced eye. He told me that on account of the blunt point of the file having pushed aside the iris, it would never again be perfect, but that if I should chance to lose my left eye, the wounded one, though imperfect, would then be very precious. "You are young and healthy," he said, "and the lost aqueous humor will be restored and the sight also to some extent; and your left eye after the inflammation has gone down and the nerve shock is overcome—you will be able to see about as well as ever, and in two or three months bid your dark room good-bye."

So I was encouraged to believe that the world was still to be left open to me. The lonely dark days of waiting were cheered by friends, many of them little children. After sufficient light could be admitted they patiently read for me, and brought great handfuls of the flowers I liked best.

As soon as I got out into Heaven's light I started on another long excursion, making haste with all my heart to store my mind with the Lord's beauty and thus be ready for any fate, light or dark. And it was from this time that my long continuous wanderings may be said to have fairly commenced.

I bade adieu to all my mechanical inventions, determined to devote the rest of my life to the study of the inventions of God. I first went home to Wisconsin, botanizing by the way, to take leave of my father and mother, brothers and sisters, all of whom were still living near Portage. I also visited the neighbors I had known as a boy, renewed my acquaintance with them after an absence of several years and bade each a formal good-bye. When they asked where I was going, I said, "Oh! I don't know—just anywhere in the wilderness southward. I have already had glorious glimpses of the Wisconsin, Iowa, Michigan, Indiana and Canada wildernesses; now I propose to go south and see something of the vegetation of the warm end of the country, and if possible wander far enough into South America to see tropical vegetation in all its palmy glory."

All the neighbors wished me well and advised me to be careful of my health, reminding me that the swamps in the south were full of malaria. I stopped overnight at the home of an old Scotch lady who had long been my friend, and was now particularly motherly in good wishes and advice. I told her that as I was sauntering along the road near sundown I heard a little bird singing. "The day's gone, The day's done." "Weel, John, my dear laddie," she replied, "your day will never be done. There is no end to the kind of studies you are engaged in, and you are sure to go on and on, but I want you to remember the fate of Hugh Miller." She was one of the finest examples I ever knew of a kind, generous, great-hearted Scotchwoman.

After all the good wishes and good-byes were over, and I had visited Fountain Lake and Hickory Hill and my first favorite gardens and ferneries, I took a thousand-mile walk to the Gulf of Mexico from Louisville, across Kentucky, Tennessee, North Carolina, Georgia and Florida.

Fever!

Muir's saunter south was intended to take him to South America, where he hoped to find the headwaters of the Amazon, build a raft, and explore the length of that mighty river to its meeting with the Atlantic. But after the following incident, described in the first of his journals kept on his travels, Muir explained that "so long a tropical trip was likely to lead through sickly places. . . I thought I had better postpone the South American excursion and go to healthy California to see its Yosemite and Big Trees and wonderful flora in general." This bout of sickness, the longest of Muir's life, was a fortuitous event for the future of the conservation movement in the United States.

October 23.

TO-DAY I REACHED THE SEA. While I was yet many miles back in the palmy woods, I caught the scent of the salt sea breeze which, although I had so many years lived far from sea breezes, suddenly conjured up Dunbar, its rocky coast, winds and waves; and my whole childhood, that seemed to have utterly vanished in the New World, was now restored amid the Florida woods by that one breath from the sea. Forgotten were the palms and magnolias and the thousand flowers that enclosed me. I could see only dulse and tangle, long-winged gulls, the

Bass Rock in the Firth of Forth, and the old castle, schools, churches, and long country rambles in search of birds' nests. I do not wonder that the weary camels coming from the scorching African deserts should be able to scent the Nile.

How imperishable are all the impressions that ever vibrate one's life! We cannot forget anything. Memories may escape the action of will, may sleep a long time, but when stirred by the right influence, though that influence be light as a shadow, they flash into full stature and life with everything in place. For nineteen years my vision was bounded by forests, but to-day, emerging from a multitude of tropical plants, I beheld the Gulf of Mexico stretching away unbounded, except by the sky. What dreams and speculative matter for thought arose as I stood on the strand, gazing out on the burnished, treeless plain!

But now at the seaside I was in difficulty. I had reached a point that I could not ford, and Cedar Keys had an empty harbor. Would I proceed down the peninsula to Tampa and Key West, where I would be sure to find a vessel for Cuba, or would I wait here, like Crusoe, and pray for a ship. Full of these thoughts, I stepped into a little store which had a considerable trade in quinine and alligator and rattlesnake skins, and inquired about shipping, means of travel, etc.

The proprietor informed me that one of several sawmills near the village was running, and that a schooner chartered to carry a load of lumber to Galveston, Texas, was expected at the mills for a load. This mill was situated on a tongue of land a few miles along the coast from Cedar Keys, and I determined to see Mr. Hodgson, the owner, to find out particulars about the expected schooner, the time she would take to load, whether I would be likely to obtain passage on her, etc.

Found Mr. Hodgson at his mill. Stated my case, and was kindly furnished the desired information. I determined to wait the two weeks likely to elapse before she sailed, and go on her to the flowery plains of Texas, from any of whose ports, I fancied, I could easily find passage to the West Indies. I agreed to work for Mr. Hodgson in the mill until I sailed, as I had but little money. He invited me to his spacious house, which occupied a shell hillock and commanded a fine view of the Gulf and many gems of palmy islets, called "keys," that fringe the shore like huge bouquets—not too big, however, for the spacious waters. Mr. Hodgson's family welcomed me with that open, unconstrained cordiality which is characteristic of the better class of Southern people.

At the sawmill a new cover had been put on the main driving pulley, which, made of rough plank, had to be turned off and smoothed. He asked me if I was able to do this job and I told him that I could. Fixing a rest and making a tool out of an old file, I directed the engineer to start the engine and run slow. After turning down the pulley and getting it true, I put a keen edge on a common carpenter's plane, quickly finished the job, and was assigned a bunk in one of the employees' lodging-houses.

The next day I felt a strange dullness and headache while I was botanizing along the coast. Thinking that a bath in the salt water might refresh me, I plunged in and swam a little distance, but this seemed only to make me feel worse. I felt anxious for something sour, and walked back to the village to buy lemons.

Thus and here my long walk was interrupted. I thought that a few days' sail would land me among the famous flower-beds of Texas. But the expected ship came and went while I was helpless with fever. The very day after reaching the sea I began to be weighed down by inexorable leaden numbness, which I resisted and tried to shake off for three days, by bathing in the Gulf, by dragging myself about among the palms, plants, and strange shells of the shore, and by doing a little mill work. I did not fear any serious illness, for I never was sick before, and was unwilling to pay attention to my feelings.

But yet heavier and more remorselessly pressed the growing fever, rapidly gaining on my strength. On the third day after my arrival I could not take any nourishment, but craved acid. Cedar Keys was only a mile or two distant, and I managed to walk there to buy lemons. On returning, about the middle of the afternoon, the fever broke on me like a storm, and before I had staggered halfway to the mill I fell down unconscious on the narrow trail among dwarf palmettos.

When I awoke from the hot fever sleep, the stars were shining, and I was at a loss to know which end of the trail to take, but fortunately, as it afterwards proved, I guessed right. Subsequently, as I fell again and again after walking only a hundred yards or so, I was careful to lie with my head in the direction in which I thought the mill was. I rose, staggered, and fell. I know not how many times, in delirious bewilderment, gasping and throbbing with only moments of consciousness. Thus passed the hours till after midnight, when I reached the mill lodging-house.

The watchman on his rounds found me lying on a heap of sawdust at the foot of the stairs. I asked him to assist me up the steps to bed, but he thought my difficulty was only intoxication and refused to help me. The mill hands, especially on Saturday nights, often returned from the village drunk. This was the cause of the watchman's refusal. Feeling that I must get to bed, I made out to reach it on hands and knees, tumbled in after a desperate struggle, and immediately became oblivious to everything.

I awoke at a strange hour on a strange day to hear Mr. Hodgson ask a watcher beside me whether I had yet spoken, and when he replied that I had not, he said: "Well, you must keep on pouring in quinine. That's all we can do." How long I lay unconscious I never found out, but it must have been many days. Some time or other I was moved on a horse from the mill quarters to Mr. Hodgson's house, where I was nursed about three months with unfailing kindness, and to the skill and care of Mr. and Mrs. Hodgson I doubtless owe my life. Through quinine and calomel—in sorry abundance—with other milder medicines, my malarial fever became typhoid. I had night sweats, and my legs became like posts of the temper and consistency of clay on account of dropsy. So on until January, a weary time.

Excerpted from *A Thousand-Mile Walk to the Gulf*, edited by William Frederic Badè. Boston and New York: Houghton Mifflin Company, 1916.

The Brink of the Yosemite Fall

Arriving in San Francisco in April of 1868, Muir wasted no time in finding his way to the top of Pacheco Pass, where he beheld for the first time his precious "range of light"—the Sierra Nevada. A few weeks later he walked into the Yosemite Valley, reluctantly departing within a week or so to find work as a shepherd in the San Joaquin Valley. In early summer of the next year, he signed on to drive a flock of sheep up the western flank of the Sierra to the Tuolumne Meadows in the Yosemite high country. This employment led him to this first investigation of the Yosemite Fall.

July 15.

FOLLOWED THE MONO TRAIL up the eastern rim of the basin nearly to its summit, then turned off southward to a small shallow valley that extends to the edge of the Yosemite, which we reached about noon, and encamped. After luncheon I made haste to high ground, and from the top of the ridge on the west side of Indian Cañon gained the noblest view of the summit peaks I have ever yet enjoyed. Nearly all the upper basin of the Merced was displayed, with its sublime domes and cañons, dark upsweeping forests, and glorious array of white peaks deep in the sky, every feature glowing, radiating beauty that pours into our flesh and bones like heat rays from fire. Sunshine over all; no breath of wind to stir the brooding calm. Never before had I seen so glorious a landscape, so boundless an affluence of sublime mountain beauty. The most extravagant description I might give of this view to any one who has not seen similar landscapes with his own eyes would not so much as hint its grandeur and the spiritual glow that covered it. I shouted and gesticulated in a wild burst of ecstasy, much to the astonishment of St. Bernard Carlo, who came running up to me, manifesting in his intelligent eyes a puzzled concern that was very ludicrous, which had the effect of bringing me to my senses. A brown bear, too, it would seem, had been a spectator of the show I had made of myself, for I had gone but a few yards when I started one from a thicket of brush. He evidently considered me dangerous, for he ran away very fast, tumbling over the tops of the tangled manzanita bushes in his haste. Carlo drew back, with his ears depressed as if afraid, and kept looking me in the face, as if expecting me to pursue and shoot, for he had seen many a bear battle in his day.

Following the ridge, which made a gradual descent to the south, I came at length to the brow of that massive cliff that stands between Indian Cañon and Yosemite Falls, and here the far-famed valley came suddenly into view throughout almost its whole extent. The noble walls—sculptured into endless variety of domes and gables, spires and battlements and plain mural precipices—all a-tremble with the thunder tones of the falling water. The level bottom seemed to be dressed like a garden—sunny meadows here and there, and groves of pine and oak; the river of Mercy sweeping in majesty through the midst of them and flashing back the sunbeams. The great Tissiack, or Half-Dome, rising at the upper end of the valley to a height of nearly a mile, is nobly proportioned and life-like, the most impressive of all the rocks, holding the eye in devout admiration, calling it back again and again from falls or meadows, or even the mountains beyond,—marvelous cliffs, marvelous in sheer dizzy depth and sculpture, types of endurance. Thousands of years have they stood in the sky exposed to rain, snow, frost, earthquake and avalanche, yet they still wear the bloom of youth.

I rambled along the valley rim to the westward; most of it is rounded off on the very brink, so that it is not easy to find places where one may look clear down the face of the wall to the bottom. When such places were found, and I had cautiously set my feet and drawn my body erect, I could not help fearing a little that the rock might split off and let me down, and what a down!—more than three thousand feet. Still my limbs did not tremble, nor did I feel the least uncertainty as to the reliance to be placed on them. My only fear was that a flake of the granite, which in some places showed joints more or less open and running parallel with the face of the cliff, might give way. After withdrawing from such places, excited with the view I had got, I would say to myself, "Now don't go out on the verge again." But in the face of Yosemite scenery cautious remonstrance is vain; under its spell one's body seems to go where it likes with a will over which we seem to have scarce any control.

After a mile or so of this memorable cliff work I approached Yosemite Creek, admiring its easy, graceful, confident gestures as it comes bravely forward in its narrow channel, singing the last of its mountain songs on its way to its fate—a few rods more over the shining granite, then down half a mile in showy foam to another world, to be lost in the

Merced, where climate, vegetation, inhabitants, all are different. Emerging from its last gorge, it glides in wide lace-like rapids down a smooth incline into a pool where it seems to rest and compose its gray, agitated waters before taking the grand plunge, then slowly slipping over the lip of the pool basin, it descends another glossy slope with rapidly accelerated speed to the brink of the tremendous cliff, and with sublime, fateful confidence springs out free in the air.

I took off my shoes and stockings and worked my way cautiously down alongside the rushing flood, keeping my feet and hands pressed firmly on the polished rock. The blooming, roaring water, rushing past close to my head was very exciting. I had expected that the sloping apron would terminate with the perpendicular wall of the valley, and that from the foot of it, where it is less steeply inclined, I should be able to lean far enough out to see the forms and behavior of the fall all the way down to the bottom. But I found that there was yet another small brow over which I could not see, and which appeared to be too steep for mortal feet. Scanning it keenly, I discovered a narrow shelf about three inches wide on the very brink, just wide enough for a rest for one's heels. But there seemed to be no way of reaching it over so steep a brow. At length, after careful scrutiny of the surface, I found an irregular edge of a flake of the rock some distance back from the margin of the torrent. If I was to get down to the brink at all that rough edge, which might offer slight finger-holds, was the only way. But the slope beside it looked dangerously smooth and steep, and the swift roaring flood beneath, overhead, and beside me was very nerve-trying. I therefore concluded not to venture farther, but did nevertheless. Tufts of artemisia were growing in clefts of the rock near by, and

I filled my mouth with the bitter leaves, hoping they might help to prevent giddiness. Then, with a caution not known in ordinary circumstances, I crept down safely to the little ledge, got my heels well planted on it, then shuffled in a horizontal direction twenty or thirty feet until close to the outplunging current, which, by the time it had descended thus far, was already white. Here I obtained a perfectly free view down into the heart of the snowy, chanting throng of comet-like streamers, into which the body of the fall soon separates.

While perched on that narrow niche I was not distinctly conscious of danger. The tremendous grandeur of the fall in form and sound and motion, acting at close range, smothered the sense of fear, and in such places one's body takes keen care for safety on its own account. How long I remained down there, or how I returned, I can hardly tell. Anyhow I had a glorious time, and got back to camp about dark, enjoying triumphant exhilaration soon followed by dull weariness. Hereafter I'll try to keep from such extravagant, nerve-straining places. Yet such a day is well worth venturing for. My first view of the High Sierra, first view looking down into Yosemite, the death song of Yosemite Creek, and its flight over the vast cliff, each one of these is of itself enough for a great life-long landscape fortune—a most memorable of days—enjoyment enough to kill if that were possible.

July 16.

My enjoyments yesterday afternoon, especially at the head of the fall, were too great for good sleep. Kept starting up last night in a nervous tremor, half awake, fancying that the foundation of the mountain we were camped on had given way and was falling into Yosemite Valley. In vain I roused myself to make a new beginning for sound sleep. The nerve strain had been too great, and again and again I dreamed I was rushing through the air above a glorious avalanche of water and rock. One time, springing to my feet, I said, "This time it is real—all must die, and where could mountaineer find a more glorious death!"

Excerpted from *My First Summer in the Sierra*. Boston and New York: Houghton Mifflin Company, 1911.

An Interview with a Bear

Muir found his employment as a sheepherder in the "Lord's grandest gardens" distasteful. The massive destruction of the high mountain meadows by the "hoofed locusts" deeply distressed him, and he found solace in his studies of the flora and fauna of the High Sierra. In this amusing "interview," Muir can be justly charged with endowing his fellow mountaineer with human qualities. While an anthropomorphic tendency is evident in much of his writing, it is not so much a mawkish sentimentality as it is a keenly-felt awareness of kinship with all of our "fellow mortals." Muir first wrote in his journal about his encounter with the bear flushed out by Carlo, and revealed that after the bear sauntered off, Muir "reluctantly went back to camp for the . . . rifle to shoot him, if necessary, in defense of the flock. Fortunately I couldn't find him. . ."

The close-up encounter with the grizzly bear took place in the Tehipite Valley, south of Yosemite. Writing of the incident in Century Magazine *in 1891, Muir said, "He came on within a dozen yards of me, and I had a good quiet look into his eyes."*

THE SIERRA BEAR, brown or gray, the sequoia of the animals, tramps over all the park, though few travelers have the pleasure of seeing him. On he fares through the majestic forests and cañons, facing all sorts of weather, rejoicing in his strength, everywhere at home, harmonizing with the trees and rocks and shaggy chaparral. Happy fellow! his lines have fallen in pleasant places,—lily gardens in silver-fir forests, miles of bushes in endless variety and exuberance of bloom over hill-waves and valleys and along the banks of streams, cañons full of music and waterfalls, parks fair as Eden,—places in which one might expect to meet angels rather than bears.

In this happy land no famine comes nigh him. All the year round his bread is sure, for some of the thousand kinds that he likes are always in season and accessible, ranged on the shelves of the mountains like stores in a pantry. From one to another, from climate to climate, up and down he climbs, feasting on each in turn,—enjoying as great variety as if he traveled to far-off countries north and south. To him almost every thing is food except granite. Every tree helps to feed him, every bush and herb, with fruits and flowers, leaves and bark; and all the animals he can catch,—badgers, gophers, ground squirrels, lizards, snakes, etc., and ants, bees, wasps, old and young, together with their eggs and larvae and nests. Craunched and hashed, down all go to his marvelous stomach, and vanish as if cast into a fire. What digestion! A sheep or a wounded deer or a pig he eats warm, about as quickly as a boy eats a buttered muffin; or should the meat be a month old, it still is welcomed with tremendous relish. After so gross a meal as this, perhaps the next will be strawberries and clover, or raspberries with mushrooms and nuts, or puckery acorns and chokecherries. And as if fearing that anything eatable in all his dominions should escape being eaten, he breaks into cabins to look after sugar, dried apples, bacon, etc. Occasionally he eats the mountaineer's bed; but when he has had a full meal of more tempting dainties he usually leaves it undisturbed, though he has been known to drag it up through a hole in the roof, carry it to the foot of a tree, and lie down on it to enjoy a siesta. Eating everything, never is he himself eaten except by man, and only man is an enemy to be feared. "B'ar meat," said a hunter from whom I was seeking information, "b'ar meat is the best meat in the mountains; their skins make the best beds, and their grease the best butter. Biscuit shortened with b'ar grease goes as far as beans; a man will walk all day on a couple of them biscuit."

In my first interview with a Sierra bear we were frightened and embarrassed, both of us, but the bear's behavior was better than mine. When I discovered him, he was standing in a narrow strip of meadow, and I was concealed behind a tree on the side of it. After studying his appearance as he stood at rest, I rushed toward him to frighten him, that I might study his gait in running. But, contrary to all I had heard about the shyness of bears, he did not run at all; and when I stopped short within a few steps of him, as he held his ground in a fighting attitude, my mistake was monstrously plain. I was then put on my good behavior, and never afterward forgot the right manners of the wilderness.

This happened on my first Sierra excursion in the forest to the north of Yosemite Valley. I was eager to meet the animals, and many of them came to me as if willing to show themselves and make my acquaintance; but the bears kept out of my way.

An old mountaineer, in reply to my questions, told me that bears were very shy, all save grim old grizzlies, and that I might travel the mountains for years without seeing one, unless I gave my mind to them and practiced the stealthy ways of hunters. Nevertheless, it was only a few weeks after I had received this information that I met the one mentioned above, and obtained instruction at first hand.

I was encamped in the woods about a mile back of the rim of Yosemite, beside a stream that falls into the valley by the way of Indian Cañon. Nearly every day for weeks I went to the top of the North Dome to sketch; for it commands a general view of the valley, and I was anxious to draw every tree and rock and waterfall. Carlo, a St. Bernard dog, was my companion,—a fine, intelligent fellow that belonged to a hunter who was compelled to remain all summer on the hot plains, and who loaned-him to me for the season for the sake of having him in the mountains, where he would be so much better off. Carlo knew bears through long experience, and he it was who led me to my first interview, though he seemed as much surprised as the bear at my unhunter-like behavior. One morning in June, just as the sunbeams began to stream through the trees, I set out for a day's sketching on the dome; and before we had gone half a mile from camp, Carlo snuffed the air and looked cautiously ahead, lowered his bushy tail, drooped his ears, and began to step softly like a cat, turning every few yards and looking me in the face with a telling expression, saying plainly enough, "There is a bear a little way ahead." I walked carefully in the indicated direction, until I approached a small flowery meadow that I was familiar with and crawled to the foot of a tree on its margin, bearing in mind what I had been told about the shyness of bears. Looking out cautiously over the instep of the tree, I saw a big, burly cinnamon bear about thirty yards off, half erect, his rear resting on the trunk of a fir that had fallen into the meadow, his hips almost buried in grass and flowers. He was listening attentively and trying to catch the scent, showing that in some way he was aware of our approach. I watched his gestures, and tried to make the most of my opportunity to learn what I could about him, fearing he would not stay long. He made a fine picture, standing alert in the sunny garden walled in by the most beautiful firs in the world.

After examining him at leisure, noting the sharp muzzle thrust inquiringly forward, the long shaggy hair on his broad chest, the stiff ears nearly buried in hair, and the slow, heavy way in which he moved his head, I foolishly made a rush on him, throwing up my arms and shouting to frighten him, to see him run. He did not mind the demonstration much; only pushed his head farther forward, and looked at me sharply as if asking, "What now? If you want to fight, I'm ready." Then I began to fear that on me would fall the work of running. But I was afraid to run, lest he should be encouraged to pursue me; therefore I held my ground, staring him in the face within a dozen yards or so, putting on as bold a look as I could, and hoping the influence of the human eye would be as great as it is said to be. Under these strained relations the interview seemed to last a long time. Finally, the bear, seeing how still I was, calmly withdrew his huge jaws from the log, gave me a piercing look, as if warning me not to follow him, turned, and walked slowly up the middle of the meadow into the forest; stopping every few steps and looking back to make sure that I was not trying to take him at a disadvantage in a rear attack. I was glad to part with him, and greatly enjoyed the vanishing view as he waded through the lilies and columbines.

Thenceforth I always tried to give bears respectful notice of my approach, and they usually kept well out of my way. Though they often came around my camp in the night, only once afterward, as far as I know, was I very near one of them in daylight. This time it was a grizzly I met; and as luck would have it, I was even nearer to him than I had been to the big cinnamon. Though not a large specimen, he seemed formidable enough at a distance of less than a dozen yards. His shaggy coat was well-grizzled, his head almost white. When I first caught sight of him he was eating acorns under a Kellogg oak, at a distance of perhaps seventy-five yards, and I tried to slip past without disturbing him. But he had either heard my steps on the gravel or caught my scent, for he came straight toward me, stopping every rod or so to look and listen: and as I was afraid to be seen running I crawled on my hands and knees a little way to one side and hid behind a libocedrus, hoping he would pass me unnoticed. He soon came up opposite me, and stood looking ahead, while I looked at him, peering past the bulging trunk of the tree. At last, turning his head, he caught sight of mine, stared sharply a minute or two, and then, with fine dignity, disappeared in a manzanita-covered earthquake talus.

Excerpted from *Our National Parks*. Boston and New York: Houghton Mifflin Company, 1901.

In the Midst of the Yosemite Fall

In the fall of 1869, Muir found on-and-off employment in the Yosemite Valley, building a sawmill, helping to erect cottages for the early tourist trade, and guiding artists, photographers and an occasional tourist party into the high country. The Valley was to be his headquarters for his Sierra Nevada explorations and studies for most of the next six years. His first cabin, built alongside the eastern edge of Yosemite Creek and just beneath the 2,425-foot Yosemite Fall, gave him easy access to Sunnyside Bench and Fern Ledge, spots from which he could study the glacially-carved Valley, and gain close-up views of the Fall.

THE BRIDAL VEIL AND VERNAL FALLS are famous for their rainbows; and special visits to them are often made when the sun shines into the spray at the most favorable angle. But amid the spray and foam and fine-ground mist ever rising from the various falls and cataracts there is an affluence and variety of iris bows scarcely known to visitors who stay only a day or two. Both day and night, winter and summer, this divine light may be seen wherever water is falling, dancing, singing; telling the heart-peace of Nature amid the wildest displays of her power. In the bright spring mornings the black-walled recess at the foot of the Lower Yosemite Fall is lavishly filled with irised spray; and not simply does this span the dashing foam, but the foam itself, the whole mass of it, beheld at a certain distance, seems to be colored, and drifts and wavers from color to color, mingling with the foliage of the adjacent trees, without suggesting any relationship to the ordinary rainbow. This is perhaps the largest and most reservoir-like fountain of iris colors to be found in the Valley.

Lunar rainbows or spray-bows also abound in the glorious affluence of dashing, rejoicing, hurrahing, enthusiastic spring floods, their colors as distinct as those of the sun and regularly and obviously banded, though less vivid. Fine specimens may be found any night at the foot of the Upper Yosemite Fall, glowing gloriously amid the gloomy shadows and thundering waters, whenever there is plenty of moonlight and spray. Even the secondary bow is at times distinctly visible.

The best point from which to observe them is on Fern Ledge. For some time after moonrise, at time of high water, the arc has a span of about five hundred feet, and is set upright; one end planted in the boiling spray at the bottom, the other in the edge of the fall, creeping lower, of course, and becoming less upright as the moon rises higher. This grand arc of color, glowing in mild, shapely beauty in so weird and huge a chamber of night shadows, and amid the rush and roar and tumultuous dashing of this thunder-voiced fall, is one of the most impressive and most cheering of all the blessed mountain evangels.

Smaller bows may be seen in the gorge on the plateau between the Upper and Lower Falls. Once toward midnight, after spending a few hours with the wild beauty of the Upper Fall, I sauntered along the edge of the gorge, looking in here and there, wherever the footing felt safe, to see what I could learn of the night aspects of the smaller falls that dwell there. And down in an exceedingly black, pit-like portion of the gorge, at the foot of the highest of the intermediate falls, into which the moonbeams were pouring through a narrow opening, I saw a well-defined spray-bow, beautifully distinct in colors, spanning the pit from side to side, while pure white foam-waves beneath the beautiful bow were constantly springing up out of the dark into the moonlight like dancing ghosts.

A wild scene, but not a safe one, is made by the moon as it appears through the edge of the Yosemite Fall when one is behind it. Once, after enjoying the night-song of the waters and watching the formation of the colored bow as the moon came round the domes and sent her beams into the wild uproar, I ventured out on the narrow bench that extends back of the fall from Fern Ledge and began to admire the dim-veiled grandeur of the view. I could see the fine gauzy threads of the fall's filmy border by having the light in front; and wishing to look at the moon through the meshes of some of the denser portions of the fall, I ventured to creep farther behind it while it was gently wind-swayed, without taking sufficient thought about the consequences of its swaying back to its natural position after the wind-pressure should be removed. The effect was enchanting: fine, savage music sounding above, beneath, around me; while the moon, apparently in the very midst of the rushing waters, seemed to be struggling to keep her place, on account of the ever-varying form and density of the water masses through which she was seen, now darkly veiled or eclipsed by a rush of thick-headed comets, now flashing out through openings between their tails. I was in fairyland between the dark wall and the wild throng of illumined waters, but suffered sudden disenchantment; for, like the witch-scene in Alloway Kirk, "in an instant all was dark." Down came a dash of spent comets, thin and harmless-looking in the distance, but they felt desperately solid and stony when they struck my shoulders, like a mixture of choking spray and gravel and big hailstones. Instinctively dropping on my knees, I gripped an angle of the rock, curled up like a young fern frond with my face pressed against my breast, and in this attitude submitted as best I could to my thundering bath. The heavier masses seemed to strike like cobblestones, and there was a confused noise of many waters about my ears—hissing, gurgling, clashing sounds that were not heard as music. The situation was quickly realized. How fast one's thoughts burn in such times of stress! I was weighing chances of escape. Would the column be swayed a few inches away from the wall, or would it come yet closer? The fall was in flood and not so lightly would its ponderous mass be swayed. My fate seemed to depend on a breath of the "idle wind." It was moved gently forward, the pounding ceased, and I was once more visited by glimpses of the moon. But fearing I might be caught at a disadvantage in making too hasty a retreat, I moved only a few feet along the bench to where a block of ice lay. I wedged myself between the ice and the wall, and lay face downwards, until the steadiness of the light gave encouragement to rise and get away. Somewhat nerve-shaken, drenched, and benumbed, I made out to build a fire, warmed myself, ran home, reached my cabin before daylight, got an hour or two of sleep, and awoke sound and comfortable, better, not worse, for my hard midnight bath.

Excerpted from *The Yosemite*. New York: The Century Co., 1912.

Climbing the Ice Cone

Most Yosemite Valley residents found Muir to be likeable enough, but eccentric, perhaps foolhardy, in his enthusiasm for long trips into the back country, for his delight in stormy weather and for his challenging investigations of natural phenomena like the ice cone.

When the first heavy storms stopped work on the high mountains, I made haste down to my Yosemite den, not to "hole up" and sleep the white months away; I was out every day, and often all night, sleeping but little, studying the so-called wonders and common things ever on show, wading, climbing, sauntering among the blessed storms and calms, rejoicing in almost everything alike that I could see or hear: the glorious brightness of frosty mornings; the sunbeams pouring over the white domes and crags into the groves and waterfalls, kindling marvelous iris fires in the hoarfrost and spray; the great forests and mountains in their deep noon sleep; the good-night alpenglow; the stars; the solemn gazing moon, drawing the huge domes and headlands one by one glowing white out of the shadows hushed and breathless like an audience in awful enthusiasm, while the meadows at their feet sparkle with frost-stars like the sky; the sublime darkness of storm-nights, when all the lights are out; the clouds in whose depths the frail snow-flowers grow; the behavior and many voices of the different kinds of storms, trees, birds, waterfalls, and snow-avalanches in the ever-changing weather.

Every clear, frosty morning loud sounds are heard booming and reverberating from side to side of the Valley at intervals of a few minutes, beginning soon after sunrise and continuing an hour or two like a thunder-storm. In my first winter in the Valley I could not make out the source of this noise. I thought of falling boulders, rock-blasting, etc. Not till I saw what looked like hoarfrost dropping from the side of the Fall was the problem explained. The strange thunder is made by the fall of sections of ice formed of spray that is frozen on the face of the cliff along the sides of the Upper Yosemite Fall—a sort of crystal plaster, a foot or two thick, cracked off by the sunbeams, awakening all the Valley like cock-crowing, announcing the finest weather, shouting aloud Nature's infinite industry and love of hard work in creating beauty.

This frozen spray gives rise to one of the most interesting winter features of the Valley—a cone of ice at the foot of the fall, four or five hundred feet high. From the Fern Ledge standpoint its crater-like throat is seen, down which the fall plunges with deep, gasping explosions of compressed air, and, after being well churned in the stormy interior, the water bursts forth through arched openings at its base, apparently scourged and weary and glad to escape, while belching spray, spouted up out of the throat past the descending current, is wafted away in irised drifts to the adjacent rocks and groves. It is built during the night and early hours of the morning; only in spells of exceptionally cold and cloudy weather is the work continued through the day. The greater part of the spray material falls in crystalline showers direct to its place, something like a small local snow-storm; but a considerable portion is first frozen on the face of the cliff along the sides of the fall and stays there until expanded and cracked off in irregular masses, some of them tons in weight, to be built into the walls of the cone; while in windy, frosty weather, when the fall is swayed from side to side, the cone is well drenched and the loose ice masses and spray-dust are all firmly welded and frozen together. Thus the finest of the downy wafts and curls of spray-dust, which in mild nights fall about as silently as dew, are held back until sunrise to make a store of heavy ice to reinforce the waterfall's thunder-tones.

While the cone is in process of formation, growing higher and wider in the frosty weather, it looks like a beautiful smooth, pure-white hill; but when it is wasting and breaking up in the spring its surface is strewn with leaves, pine branches, stones, sand, etc., that have been brought over the fall, making it look like a heap of avalanche detritus.

Anxious to learn what I could about the structure of this curious hill I often approached it in calm weather and tried to climb it, carrying an ax to cut steps. Once I nearly succeeded in gaining the summit. At the base I was met by a current of spray and wind that made seeing and breathing difficult. I pushed on backward, however, and soon gained the slope of the hill, where by creeping close to the surface most of the choking blast passed over me and I managed to crawl up with but little difficulty. Thus I made my way nearly to the summit, halting at times to peer up through the wild whirls of spray at the veiled grandeur of the fall, or to listen to the thunder beneath me; the whole hill was sounding as if it were a huge, bellowing drum. I hoped that by waiting until the fall was blown aslant I should be able to climb to the lip of the crater and get a view of the interior; but a suffocating blast, half air, half water, followed by the fall of an enormous mass of frozen spray from a spot high up on the wall, quickly discouraged me. The whole cone was jarred by the blow and some fragments of the mass sped past me dangerously near; so I beat a hasty retreat, chilled and drenched, and lay down on a sunny rock to dry.

Once during a wind-storm when I saw that the fall was frequently blown westward, leaving the cone dry, I ran up to Fern Ledge hoping to gain a clear view of the interior. I set out at noon. All the way up the storm notes were so loud about me that the voice of the fall was almost drowned by them. Notwithstanding the rocks and bushes everywhere were drenched by the wind-driven spray, I approached the brink of the precipice overlooking the mouth of the ice cone, but I was almost suffocated by the drenching, gusty spray, and was compelled to seek shelter. I searched for some hiding-place in the wall from whence I might run out at some opportune moment when the fall with its whirling spray and torn shreds of comet tails and trailing, tattered skirts was borne westward, as I had seen it carried several times before, leaving the cliffs on the east side and the ice hill bare in the sunlight. I had not long to wait, for, as if ordered so for my special accommodation, the mighty downrush of comets with their whirling drapery swung westward and remained aslant for nearly half an hour. The cone was admirably lighted and deserted by the water, which fell most of the time on the rocky western slopes mostly outside of the cone. The mouth into which the fall pours was, as near as I could guess, about one hundred feet in diameter north and south and about two hundred feet east and west, which is about the shape and size of the fall at its best in its normal condition at this season.

The crater-like opening was not a true oval, but more like a huge coarse mouth. I could see down the throat about one hundred feet or perhaps farther.

The fall precipice overhangs from a height of 400 feet above the base; therefore the water strikes some distance from the base of the cliff, allowing space for the accumulation of a considerable mass of ice between the fall and the wall.

Excerpted from *The Yosemite*. New York: The Century Co., 1912.

The Snow Avalanche Ride

As a Yosemite Valley resident, Muir made many winter excursions to the top of the Valley walls in all kinds of weather to see "what was going on." Most of Muir's adventures can be geographically pinpointed, but the specific "side canyon" that he climbed here has never been identified.

THE FIRST OF THE GREAT SNOW-STORMS that replenish the Yosemite fountains seldom sets in before the end of November. Then, warned by the sky, wide-awake mountaineers, together with the deer and most of the birds, make haste to the lowlands or foothills; and burrowing marmots, mountain beavers, wood-rats, and other small mountain people, go into winter quarters, some of them not again to see the light of day until the general awakening and resurrection of the spring in June or July. The fertile clouds, drooping and condensing in brooding silence, seem to be thoughtfully examining the forests and streams with reference to the work that lies before them. At length, all their plans perfected, tufted flakes and single starry crystals come in sight, solemnly swirling and glinting to their blessed appointed places; and soon the busy throng fills the sky and makes darkness like night. The first heavy fall is usually from about two to four feet in depth; then with intervals of days or weeks of bright weather storm succeeds storm, heaping snow on snow, until thirty to fifty feet has fallen. But on account of its settling and compacting, and waste from melting and evaporation, the average depth actually found at any time seldom exceeds ten feet in the forest regions, or fifteen feet along the slopes of the summit peaks. After snow-storms come avalanches, varying greatly in form, size, behavior and in the songs they sing; some on the smooth slopes of the mountains are short and broad; others long and river-like in the side cañons of yosemites and in the main cañons, flowing in regular channels and booming like waterfalls, while countless smaller ones fall everywhere from laden trees and rocks and lofty cañon walls. Most delightful it is to stand in the middle of Yosemite on still clear mornings after snow-storms and watch the throng of avalanches as they come down, rejoicing, to their places, whispering, thrilling like birds, or booming and roaring like thunder. The noble yellow pines stand hushed and motionless as if under a spell until the morning sunshine begins to sift through their laden spires; then the dense masses on the ends of the leafy branches begin to shift and fall, those from the upper branches striking the lower ones in succession, enveloping each tree in a hollow conical avalanche of fairy fineness; while the relieved branches spring up and wave with startling effect in the general stillness, as if each tree was moving of its own volition. Hundreds of broad cloud-shaped masses may also be seen, leaping over the brows of the cliffs from great heights, descending at first with regular avalanche speed until, worn into dust by friction, they float in front of the precipices like irised clouds. Those which descend from the brow of El Capitan are particularly fine; but most of the great Yosemite avalanches flow in regular channels like cascades and waterfalls.

When the snow first gives way on the upper slopes of their basins, a dull rushing, rumbling sound is heard which rapidly increases and seems to draw nearer with appalling intensity of tone. Presently the white flood comes bounding into sight over bosses and sheer places, leaping from bench to bench, spreading and narrowing and throwing off clouds of whirling dust like the spray of foaming cataracts. Compared with waterfalls and cascades, avalanches are short-lived, few of them lasting more than a minute or two, and the sharp, clashing sounds so common in falling water are mostly wanting; but in their low massy thundertones and purple-tinged whiteness, and in their dress, gait, gestures and general behavior, they are much alike.

Besides these common after-storm avalanches that are to be found not only in the Yosemite but in all the deep, sheer-walled cañons of the Range there are two other important kinds, which may be called annual and century avalanches, which still further enrich the scenery. The only place about the Valley where one may be sure to see the annual kind is on the north slope of Clouds' Rest. They are composed of heavy, compacted snow, which has been subjected to frequent alternations of freezing and thawing. They are developed on cañon and mountain-sides at an elevation of from nine to ten thousand feet, where the slopes are inclined at an angle too low to shed off the dry winter snow, and which accumulates until the spring thaws sap their foundations and make them slippery; then away in grand style go the ponderous icy masses without any fine snow-dust. Those of Clouds' Rest descend like thunderbolts for more than a mile.

The great century avalanches and the kind that mow wide swaths through the upper forests occur on mountain-sides about ten or twelve thousand feet high, where under ordinary weather conditions the snow accumulated from winter to winter lies at rest for many years, allowing trees, fifty to a hundred feet high, to grow undisturbed on the slopes beneath them. On their way down through the woods they seldom fail to make a perfectly clean sweep, stripping off the soil as well as the trees, clearing paths two or three hundred yards wide from the timber line to the glacier meadows or lakes, and piling their uprooted trees, head downward, in rows along the sides of the gaps like lateral moraines. Scars and broken branches of the trees standing on the sides of the gaps record the depth of the overwhelming flood; and when we come to count the annual wood-rings on the uprooted trees we learn that some of these immense avalanches occur only once in a century or even at still wider intervals.

Few Yosemite visitors ever see snow avalanches and fewer still know the exhilaration of riding on them. In all my mountaineering I have enjoyed only one avalanche ride, and the start was so sudden and the end came so soon I had but little time to think of the danger that attends this sort of travel, though at such times one thinks fast. One fine Yosemite morning after a heavy snowfall, being eager to see as many avalanches as possible and wide views of the forest and summit peaks in their new white robes before the sunshine had time to change them, I set out early to climb by a side cañon to the top of a commanding ridge a little over three thousand feet above the Valley. On account of the looseness of the snow that blocked the cañon I knew the climb would require a long time, some three or four hours as I estimated; but it proved far more difficult than I had anticipated. Most of the way I sank waist deep, almost out of sight in some places. After spending the whole day to within half an hour or so of sundown, I was still several hundred feet below the summit. Then my hopes were reduced to getting up in time to see the sunset. But I was not to get summit views of any sort that day, for deep trampling near the cañon head, where the snow was strained, started an avalanche, and I was swished down to the foot of the cañon as if by enchantment. The wallowing ascent had taken nearly all day, the descent only about a minute. When the avalanche started I threw myself on my back and spread my arms to try to keep from sinking. Fortunately, though the grade of the cañon is very steep, it is not interrupted by precipices large enough to cause outbounding or free plunging. On no part of the rush was I buried. I was only moderately imbedded on the surface or at times a little below it, and covered with a veil of back-streaming dust particles; and as the whole mass beneath and about me joined in the flight there was no friction, though I was tossed here and there and lurched from side to side. When the avalanche swedged and came to rest I found myself on top of the crumpled pile without a bruise or scar. This was a fine experience. Hawthorne says somewhere that steam has spiritualized travel; though unspiritual smells, smoke, etc, still attend steam travel. This flight in what might be called a milky way of snow-stars was the most spiritual and exhilarating of all the modes of motion I have ever experienced. Elijah's flight in a chariot of fire could hardly have been more gloriously exciting.

Excerpted from *The Yosemite*. New York: The Century Co., 1912.

Rattlesnakes

Despite an early prejudice against them, Muir's encounters with rattlesnakes (once with his face only a foot away from fangs) eventually taught him "that scales may cover as fine a nature as hair or feathers or anything tailored." He also was quick to recognize the value of snakes to agricultural interests in the Central Valley of California, knowing that they were providing efficient rodent control.

THERE ARE MANY SNAKES IN THE CAÑONS and lower forests, but they are mostly handsome and harmless. Of all the tourists and travelers who have visited Yosemite, and the adjacent mountains, not one has been bitten by a snake of any sort, while thousands have been charmed by them. Some of them vie with the lizards in beauty of color and dress patterns. Only the rattlesnake is venomous, and he carefully keeps his venom to himself as far as man is concerned unless his life is threatened.

Before I learned to respect rattlesnakes I killed two, the first on the San Joaquin plain. He was coiled comfortably around a tuft of bunchgrass, and I discovered him when he was between my feet as I was stepping over him. He held his head down and did not attempt to strike, although in danger of being trampled. At that time, thirty years ago, I imagined that rattlesnakes should be killed wherever found. I had no weapon of any sort, and on the smooth plain there was not a stick or stone within miles; so I crushed him by jumping on him, as the deer are said to do. Looking me in the face he saw I meant mischief, and quickly cast himself into a coil, ready to strike in defense. I knew he could not strike when traveling, therefore I threw handfuls of dirt and grass sods at him, to tease him out of coil. He held his ground a few minutes, threatening and striking, and then started off to get rid of me. I ran forward and jumped on him; but he drew back his head so quickly my heel missed, and he also missed his stroke at me. Persecuted, tormented, again and again he tried to get away, bravely striking out to protect himself; but at last my heel came squarely down, sorely wounding him, and a few more brutal stampings crushed him. I felt degraded by the killing business, farther from heaven, and I made up my mind to try to be at least as fair and charitable as the snakes themselves, and to kill no more save in self-defense.

The second killing might also, I think, have been avoided, and I have always felt somewhat sore and guilty about it. I had built a little cabin in Yosemite, and for convenience in getting water, and for the sake of music and society, I led a small stream from Yosemite Creek into it. Running along the side of the wall it was not in the way, and it had just fall enough to ripple and sing in low, sweet tones, making delightful company, especially at night when I was lying awake. Then a few frogs came in and made merry with the stream,—and one snake, I suppose to catch the frogs.

Returning from my long walks, I usually brought home a large handful of plants, partly for study, partly for ornament, and set them in a corner of the cabin, with their stems in the stream to keep them fresh. One day, when I picked up a handful that had begun to fade, I uncovered a large coiled rattler that had been hiding behind the flowers. Thus suddenly brought to light face to face with the rightful owner of the place, the poor reptile was desperately embarrassed, evidently realizing that he had no right in the cabin. It was not only fear that he showed, but a good deal of downright bashfulness and embarrassment, like that of a more than half honest person caught under suspicious circumstances behind a door. Instead of striking or threatening to strike, though coiled and ready, he slowly drew his head down as far as he could, with awkward, confused kinks in his neck and a shamefaced expression, as if wishing the ground would open and hide him. I have looked into the eyes of so many animals that I feel sure I did not mistake the feelings of this unfortunate snake. I did not want to kill him, but I had many visitors, some of them children, and I oftentimes came in late at night; so I judged he must die.

Since then I have seen perhaps a hundred or more in these mountains, but I have never intentionally disturbed them, nor have they disturbed me to any great extent, even by accident, though in danger of being stepped on. Once, while I was on my knees kindling a fire, one glided under the arch made by my arm. He was only going away from the ground I had selected for a camp, and there was not the slightest danger, because I kept still and allowed him to go in peace. The only time I felt myself in serious danger was when I was coming out of the Tuolumne Cañon by a steep side cañon toward the head of Yosemite Creek. On an earthquake talus, a boulder in my way presented a front so high that I could just reach the upper edge of it while standing on the next below it. Drawing myself up, as soon as my head was above the flat top of it I caught sight of a coiled rattler. My hands had alarmed him, and he was ready for me; but even with this provocation, and when my head came in sight within a foot of him, he did not strike. The last time I sauntered through the big cañon I saw about two a day. One was not coiled, but neatly folded in a narrow place between two cobblestones on the side of the river, his head below the level of them, ready to shoot up like a Jack-in-the-box for frogs or birds. My foot spanned the space above within an inch or two of his head, but he only held it lower. In making my way through a particularly tedious tangle of buckthorn, I parted the branches on the side of an open spot and threw my bundle of bread into it; and then, with my arms free, I was pushing through after it, I saw a small rattlesnake dragging his tail from beneath my bundle. When he caught sight of me he eyed me angrily, and with an air of righteous indignation seemed to be asking why I had thrown that stuff on him. He was so small that I was inclined to slight him, but he struck out so angrily that I drew back, and approached the opening from the other side. But he had been listening, and when I looked through the brush I found him confronting me, still with a come-in-if-you dare expression. In vain I tried to explain that I only wanted my bread; he stoutly held the ground in front of it; so I went back a dozen rods and kept still for half an hour, and when I returned he had gone.

One evening, near sundown, in a very rough, boulder-choked portion of the cañon, I searched long for a level spot for a bed, and at last was glad to find a patch of flood-sand on the riverbank, and a lot of driftwood close by for a campfire. But when I threw down my bundle, I found two snakes in possession of the ground. I might have passed the night even in this snake den without danger, for I never knew a single instance of their coming into camp in the night; but fearing that, in so small a space, some late comers, not aware of my presence, might get stepped on when I was replenishing the fire, to avoid possible crowding I encamped on one of the earthquake boulders.

Excerpted from *Our National Parks*. Boston and New York: Houghton Mifflin and Company, 1901.

The Earthquake

On the night of March 26, 1872, a stupendous earthquake, quite likely as large as any since in California, struck the east side of the Sierra Nevada. Muir was spending the winter caretaking Black's Hotel, located just beneath Sentinel Rock in Yosemite Valley. The Eagle Rock was just up the Valley, on the south side.

THE AVALANCHE TALUSES, leaning against the walls at intervals of a mile or two, are among the most striking and interesting of the secondary features of the Valley. They are from about three to five hundred feet high, made up of huge angular, well-preserved, unshifting boulders, and instead of being slowly weathered from the cliffs like ordinary taluses, they were all formed suddenly and simultaneously by a great earthquake that occurred at least three centuries ago. And though thus hurled into existence in a few seconds or minutes, they are the least changeable of all the Sierra soil-beds. Excepting those which were launched directly into the channels of swift rivers scarcely one of their wedged and interlacing boulders has moved since the day of their creation; and though mostly made up of huge blocks of granite, many of them from ten to fifty feet cube, weighing thousands of tons with only a few small chips, trees and shrubs make out to live and thrive on them and even delicate herbaceous plants—draperia, collomia, zauschneria, etc., soothing and coloring their wild rugged slopes with gardens and groves.

I was long in doubt on some points concerning the origin of these taluses. Plainly enough they were derived from the cliffs above them, because they are of the size of scars on the wall, the rough angular surface of which contrasts with the rounded glaciated, unfractured parts. It was plain too that instead of being made up of material slowly and gradually weathered front the cliffs like ordinary taluses, almost every one of them had been formed suddenly in a single avalanche, and had not been increased in size during the last three or four centuries, for trees three or four hundred years old are growing on them, some standing at the top close to the wall without a bruise or broken branch, showing that scarcely a single boulder had ever fallen among them. Furthermore all these taluses throughout the Range seemed by the trees and lichens growing on them to be of the same age. All the phenomena thus pointed straight to a grand ancient earthquake. But for years I left the question open, and went on from canyon to canyon, observing again and again; measuring the heights of taluses throughout the Range on both flanks, and the variations in the angles of their surface slopes; studying the way their boulders had been assorted and related and brought to rest, and their correspondence in size with the cleavage of the cliffs from whence they were derived, cautious about making up my mind. But at last all doubt as to their formation vanished.

At half-past two o'clock of a moonlit morning in March, I was awakened by a tremendous earthquake, and though I had never before enjoyed a storm of this sort, the strange thrilling motion could not be mistaken, and I ran out of my cabin, both glad and frightened, shouting, "A noble earthquake! A noble earthquake!" feeling sure I was going to learn something. The shocks were so violent and varied and succeeded one another so closely, that I had to balance myself carefully in walking as if on the deck of a ship among waves, and it seemed impossible that the high cliffs of the Valley could escape being shattered. In particular, I feared that the sheer-fronted Sentinel Rock, towering above my cabin would be shaken down, and I took shelter back of a large yellow pine, hoping that it might protect me from at least the smaller outbounding boulders. For a minute or two the shocks became more and more violent—flashing horizontal thrusts mixed with a few twists and battering explosive upheaving jolts,—as if Nature were wrecking her Yosemite temple, and getting ready to build a still better one.

I was now convinced before a single boulder had fallen that earthquakes were the talus-makers and positive proof soon came. It was a calm moonlight night, and no sound was heard for the first minute or so, save low, muffled underground, bubbling rumblings, and the whispering and rustling of the agitated trees, as if Nature were holding her breath. Then, suddenly, out of the strange silence and strange motion there came a tremendous roar. The Eagle Rock on the south wall, about a half a mile up the Valley, gave way and I saw it falling in thousands of the great boulders I had so long been studying, pouring to the Valley floor in a free curve luminous from friction, making a terribly sublime spectacle—an arc of glowing, passionate fire, fifteen hundred feet span, as true in form and as serene in beauty as a rainbow in the midst of the stupendous roaring rock-storm. The sound was so tremendously deep and broad and earnest, the whole earth like a living creature seemed to have at last found a voice and to be calling to her sister planets. In trying to tell something of the size of this awful sound it seems to me that if all the thunder of all the storms I had ever heard were condensed into one roar it would not equal this rock-roar at the birth of a mountain talus. Think, then, of the roar that arose to heaven at the simultaneous birth of all the thousands of ancient canyon-taluses throughout the length and breadth of the Range!

The first severe shocks were soon over and eager to examine the new-born talus I ran up the Valley in the moonlight and climbed upon it before the huge blocks after their fiery flight had come to complete rest. They were slowly settling into their places, chafing, grating against one another, groaning, and whispering; but no motion was visible except in a stream of small fragments pattering down the face of the cliff. A cloud of dust particles, lighted by the moon, floated out across the whole breadth of the Valley, forming a ceiling that lasted until after sunrise, and the air was filled with the odor of crushed Douglas spruces from a grove that had been mowed down and mashed like weeds.

After the ground began to calm I ran across the meadow to the river to see in what direction it was flowing and was glad to find that *down* the Valley was still down. Its waters were muddy from portions of its bank having given way, but it was flowing around its curves and over its ripples and shallows with ordinary tones and gestures. The mud would soon be cleared away and the raw slips on the banks would be the only visible record of the shaking it suffered.

The Upper Yosemite Fall, glowing white in the moonlight, seemed to know nothing of the earthquake, manifesting no change in form or voice as far as I could see or hear.

After a second startling shock, about half-past three o'clock, the ground continued to tremble gently, and smooth, hollow rumbling sounds, not always distinguishable from the rounded, bumping, explosive tones of the falls, came from deep in the mountains in a northern direction.

The few Indians fled from their huts to the middle of the Valley, fearing that angry spirits were trying to kill them; and as I afterward learned, most of the Yosemite tribe, who were spending the winter at their village on Bull Creek forty miles away, were so terrified that they ran into the river and washed themselves,—getting themselves clean enough to say their prayers, I suppose, or to die. I asked Dick, one of the Indians with whom I was acquainted, "What made the ground shake and jump so much?" He only shook his head and said, "No good. No good," and looked appealingly to me to give him hope that his life was to be spared.

In the morning I found the few white settlers assembled in front of the old Hutchings Hotel comparing notes and meditating flight to the lowlands, seemingly as sorely frightened as the Indians. Shortly after sunrise a low, blunt, muffled rumbling, like distant thunder, was followed by another series of shocks, which, though not nearly so severe as the first, made the cliffs and domes tremble like jelly, and the big pines and oaks thrill and swish and wave their branches with startling effect. Then the talkers were suddenly hushed, and the solemnity on their faces was sublime. One in particular of these winter neighbors, a somewhat speculative thinker with whom I had often conversed, was a firm believer in the cataclysmic origin of the Valley; and I now jokingly remarked that his wild tumble-down-and-engulfment hypothesis might soon be proved, since these underground rumblings and shakings might be the forerunners of another Yosemite-making cataclysm, which would perhaps double the depth of the Valley by swallowing the floor, leaving the ends of the roads and trails dangling three or four thousand feet in the air. Just then came the third series of shocks, and it was fine to see how awfully silent and solemn he became. His belief in the existence of a mysterious abyss, into which the suspended floor of the Valley and all the domes and battlements of the walls might at any moment go roaring down, mightily troubled him. To diminish his fears and laugh him into something like reasonable faith, I said, "Come, cheer up; smile a little and clap your hands, now that kind Mother Earth is trotting us on her knee to amuse us and make us good." But the well-meant joke seemed irreverent and utterly failed, as if only prayerful terror could rightly belong to the wild beauty-making business. Even after all the heavier shocks were over I could do nothing to reassure him. On the contrary, he handed me the keys of his little store to keep, saying that with a companion of like mind he was going to the lowlands to stay until the fate of poor, trembling Yosemite was settled. In vain I rallied them on their fears, calling attention to the strength of the granite walls of our Valley home, the very best and solidest masonry in the world, and less likely to collapse than the sedimentary lowlands to which they were looking for safety; and saying that in any case they sometime would have to die, and so grand a burial was not to be slighted. But they were too seriously panic-stricken to get comfort from anything I could say.

During the third severe shock the trees were so violently shaken that the birds flew out with frightened cries. In particular I noticed two robins flying in terror from a leafless oak, the branches of which swished and quivered as if struck by a heavy battering-ram. Exceedingly interesting were the flashing and quivering of the elastic needles of the pines in the sunlight and the waving up and down of the branches while the trunks stood rigid. There was no swaying, waving or swirling as in windstorms, but quick, quivering jerks, and at times the heavy tasseled branches moved as if they had all been pressed down against the trunk and suddenly let go, to spring up and vibrate until they came to rest again. Only the owls seemed to be undisturbed. Before the rumbling echoes had died away a hollow-voiced owl began to hoot in philosophical tranquillity from near the edge of the new talus as if nothing extraordinary had occurred, although, perhaps he was curious to know what all the noise was about. His "hoot-too-hoot-too-whoo" might have meant, "what's a' the steer, kimmer?"

It was long before the Valley found perfect rest. The rocks trembled more or less every day for over two months, and I kept a bucket of water on my table to learn what I could of the movements. The blunt thunder in the depths of the mountains was usually followed by sudden jarring, horizontal thrusts from the northward, often succeeded by twisting, upjolting movements. More than a month after the first great shock, when I was standing on a fallen tree up the Valley near Lamon's winter cabin, I heard a distinct bubbling thunder from the direction of Tenaya Cañon. Carlo, a large intelligent St. Bernard dog standing beside me seemed greatly astonished, and looked intently in that direction with mouth open and uttered a low *Wouf!* as if saying "What's that?" He must have known that it was not thunder though like it. The air was perfectly still, not the faintest breath of wind perceptible, and a fine, mellow, sunny hush pervaded everything in the midst of which came that subterranean thunder. Then, while we gazed and listened, came the corresponding shocks, distinct as if some mighty hand had shaken the ground. After the sharp horizontal jars died away, they were followed by a gentle rocking and undulating of the ground so distinct that Carlo looked at the log on which he was standing to see who was shaking it. It was the season of flooded meadows and the pools about me, calm as sheets of glass, were suddenly thrown into low ruffling waves.

Judging by its effects, this Yosemite, or Inyo earthquake, as it is sometimes called, was gentle as compared with the one that gave rise to the grand talus system of the Range and did so much for the canon scenery. Nature, usually so deliberate in her operations, then created, as we have seen, a new set of features simply by giving the mountains a shake—changing not only the high peaks and cliffs, but the streams. As soon as these rock avalanches fell, the streams began to sing new songs; for in many places thousands of boulders were hurled into their channels roughening and half damming them, compelling the waters to surge and roar in rapids changed to meadows through which the streams are now silently meandering; while at the same time some of the taluses took the places of old meadows and groves. Thus rough places were made smooth, and smooth places rough. But, on the whole, by what at first sight seemed pure confounded confusion and ruin, the landscapes were enriched; for gradually every talus was covered with groves and gardens and made a finely proportioned and ornamental base for the cliffs. In this work of beauty, every boulder is prepared and measured and put in its place more thoughtfully than are the stones of temples. If for a moment you are inclined to regard these taluses as mere draggled, chaotic dumps, climb to the top of one of them, and run down without any haggling, puttering hesitation, boldly jumping from boulder to boulder with even speed. You will then find your feet playing a tune, and quickly discover the music and poetry of these magnificent rock piles—a fine lesson; and all Nature's wildness tells the same story—the shocks and outbursts of earthquakes, volcanoes, geysers, roaring, thundering waves and floods, the silent uprush of sap in plants, storms of every sort—each and all are the orderly beauty-making love-beats of Nature's heart.

Excerpted from *The Yosemite*. New York: The Century Co., 1912.

The Ascent of Mount Ritter

It is not clear just how many first ascents Muir made in the Sierra Nevada, but Mount Ritter, climbed in the fall of 1872, was certainly among the most challenging. The artist Muir described as an impulsive young Scotchman cavorting "like a madman" was William Keith, soon to be a well-known painter of California landscapes. Despite Muir's humorous comments on Keith's "curious troubles" as a novice mountaineer, they were to develop a close and lifelong friendship.

Early one bright morning in the middle of Indian summer, while the glacier meadows were still crisp with frost crystals, I set out from the foot of Mount Lyell, on my way down to Yosemite Valley. I had spent the past summer, and many preceding ones, exploring the glaciers that lie on the headwaters of the San Joaquin, Tuolumne, Merced, and Owen's rivers; measuring and studying their movements, trends, crevasses, moraines, etc., and the part they had played during the period of their greater extension in the creation and development of the landscapes of this Alpine wonderland. Having been cold and hungry so many times, and worked so hard, I was weary, and began to look forward with delight to the approaching winter, when I would be warmly snow-bound in my

Yosemite cabin, with plenty of bread and books; but a tinge of regret came on when I considered that possibly I was now looking on all this fresh wilderness for the last time.

* * *

Pursuing my lonely way down the valley, I turned again and again to gaze on the glorious picture, throwing up my arms to inclose it as in a frame. After long ages of growth in the darkness beneath the glaciers, through sunshine and storms, it seemed now to be ready and waiting for the elected artist, like yellow wheat for the reaper; and I could not help wishing that I were that artist. I had to be content, however, to take it into my soul. At length, after rounding a precipitous headland that puts out from the west wall of the valley, every peak over the divide between the waters of the Merced and Tuolumne, and down through the lower forests that clothe the slopes of Cloud's Rest, arriving in Yosemite in due time—which, with me, is *any* time. And, strange to say, among the first human beings I met here were two artists who were awaiting my return. Handing me letters of introduction, they inquired whether in the course of my explorations in the adjacent mountains I had ever come upon a landscape suitable for a large painting; whereupon I began a description of the one that had so lately excited my admiration. Then, as I went on further and further into details, their faces began to glow, and I offered to guide them to it, while they declared they would gladly follow, far or near, whithersoever I could spare the time to lead them.

Since storms might come breaking down through the fine weather at any time, burying the meadow colors in snow, and cutting off their retreat, I advised getting ready at once.

Our course lay out of the valley by the Vernal and Nevada Falls, thence over the main dividing ridge to the Big Tuolumne Meadows, by the old Mono trail, and thence along the river-bank to its head.

* * *

At length, toward the end of the second day, the Sierra crown began to come into view, and when we had fairly rounded the projecting headland mentioned above, the whole picture stood revealed in the full flush of the alpenglow. Now their enthusiasm was excited beyond bounds, and the more impulsive of the two dashed ahead, shouting and gesticulating and tossing his arms in the air like a madman. Here, at last, was a typical Alpine landscape.

After feasting awhile, I proceeded to make camp in a sheltered grove a little way back from the meadow, where pine-boughs could be obtained for beds, while the artists ran here and there, along the river-bends and up the side of the cañon, choosing foregrounds for sketches. After dark, when our tea was made and a rousing fire kindled, we began to make our plans. They decided to remain here several days, at the least, while I concluded to make an excursion in the meantime to the untouched summit of Ritter.

It was now about the middle of October, the spring-time of snow-flowers. The first winter clouds had bloomed, and the peaks were strewn with fresh crystals, without, however, affecting the climbing to any dangerous extent. And as the weather was still profoundly calm, and the distance to the foot of the mountain only a little more than a day, I felt that I was running no great risk of being storm-bound.

Ritter is king of our Alps, and had never been climbed. I had explored the adjacent peaks summer after summer, and, but for the tendency to reserve a grand masterpiece like this for a special attempt, it seemed strange that in all these years I had made no effort to reach its commanding summit. Its height above sea level is about 13,300 feet, and is fenced round by steeply inclined glaciers, and cañons of tremendous depth and ruggedness, rendering it comparatively inaccessible. But difficulties of this kind only exhilarate the mountaineer.

Next morning, the artists went heartily to their work and I to mine.

* * *

My general plan was simply this: to scale the cañon wall, cross over to the eastern flank of the range, and then make my way southward to the northern spurs of Mount Ritter, in compliance with the intervening topography; for to push on directly southward from camp through the innumerable peaks and pinnacles that adorn this portion of the axis of the range is simply impossible.

* * *

Before I had gone a mile from camp, I came to the foot of a white cascade that beats its way down a rugged gorge in the cañon wall, from a height of about nine hundred feet, and pours its throbbing waters into the Tuolumne. . . .Gladly I climbed along its dashing border, absorbing its divine music, and bathing from time to time in waftings of irised spray. Climbing higher, higher, new beauty came streaming on the sight: painted meadows, late-blooming gardens, peaks of rare architecture, lakes here and there, shining like silver, and glimpses of the forested lowlands seen far in the west. Over the summit, I saw the so-called Mono desert lying dreamily silent in the thick, purple light—a desert of heavy sun-glare beheld from a desert of ice-burnished granite. Here the mountain waters divide, flowing east to vanish in the volcanic sands and dry sky of the Great Basin; west, to flow through the Golden Gate to the sea.

Passing a little way down over the summit until I had reached an elevation of about ten thousand feet, I pushed on southward toward a group of savage peaks that stand guard around Ritter on the north and west, groping my way, and dealing instinctively with every obstacle as it presented itself. Here a huge gorge would be found cutting across my path, along the dizzy edge of which I scrambled until some less precipitous point was discovered where I might safely venture to the bottom and, selecting some feasible portion of the opposite wall, re-ascend with the same slow caution. Massive, flat-topped spurs alternate with the gorges, plunging abruptly from the shoulders of the snowy peaks, and planting their feet in the warm desert. These were everywhere marked and adorned with characteristic sculptures of the ancient glaciers that swept over this entire region like one vast ice-wind, and the polished surfaces produced by the ponderous flood are still so perfectly preserved that in many places the sunlight reflected from them is about as trying to the eyes as sheets of snow.

* * *

Now came the solemn, silent evening. Long, blue, spiky-edged shadows crept out across the snow-fields, while a rosy glow, at first scarce discernible, gradually deepened and suffused every mountain-top, flushing the glaciers and the harsh crags above them. This was the alpenglow, to me the most impressive of all the terrestrial manifestations of God. At the touch of this divine light, the mountains seemed to kindle to a rapt, religious consciousness, and stood hushed like devout worshippers waiting to be blessed. Just before the alpenglow began to fade, two crimson clouds came streaming across the summit like wings of flame, rendering the sublime scene yet more intensely impressive; then came darkness and the stars.

Ritter was still miles away, but I could proceed no further that night. I found a good camp-ground on the rim of a glacier basin about 11,000 feet above the sea. A small lake nestles in the bottom of it, from which I got water for my tea, and a storm-beaten thicket nearby furnished abundance of rousing fire-wood. Somber peaks, hacked and shattered, circled half-way around the horizon, wearing a most savage aspect in the gloaming, and a water-fall chanted solemnly across the lake on its way down from the foot of a glacier.

* * *

I made my bed in a nook of the pine thicket, where the branches were pressed and crinkled overhead like a roof, and bent down around the sides. These are the best bed-chambers our Alps afford—snug as squirrel-nests, well ventilated, full of spicy odors, and with plenty of wind-played needles to sing one asleep. I little expected company, but, creeping in through a low side door, I found five or six birds nestling among the tassels. The night wind began to blow soon after dark; at first, only a gentle breathing, but increasing toward midnight to violent gale that fell upon my leafy roof in ragged surges, like a cascade, and bearing strange sounds from the crags overhead. The water-fall sang in chorus, filling the old ice-fountain with its solemn roar, and seeming to increase in power as the night advanced—fit voice for such a landscape. I had to creep out many times to the fire during the night; for it was biting cold and I had no blankets. Gladly I welcomed the morning star.

The dawn in the dry, wavering air of the desert was glorious. Everything encouraged my undertaking and betokened success. No cloud in the sky, no storm-tone in the wind. Breakfast of bread and tea was soon made. I fastened a hard, durable crust to my belt by way of provision, in case I should be compelled to pass a night on the mountain-top; then, securing the remainder of my little stock from wolves and wood-rats, I set forth free and hopeful.

* * *

On the southern shore of a frozen lake, I encountered an extensive field of hard, granular snow, up which I scampered in fine tone, intending to follow it to its head, and cross the rocky spur against which it leans, hoping thus to come direct upon the base of the main Ritter peak. The surface was pitted with oval hollows, made by stones and drift pine-needles that had melted themselves into the mass by the radiation of absorbed sun heat. These afforded good footholds, but the surface curved more and more steeply at the head, and the pits became shallower and less abundant, until I found myself in danger of being shed off like avalanching snow. I persisted, however, creeping on all fours, and shuffling up the smoothest places on my back, as I had often done on burnished granite, until, after slipping several times, I was compelled to retrace my course to the bottom, and make my way around the west end of the lake, and thence up to the summit of the divide between the head-waters of Rush Creek and the northernmost tributaries of the San Joaquin.

Arriving on the summit of this dividing crest, one of the most exciting pieces of pure wildness was disclosed that the eye of man had ever beheld. There, immediately in front, loomed the majestic mass of Mount Ritter, with a glacier swooping down its face nearly to my feet, then curving westward and pouring its frozen flood into a dark blue lake, whose shores were bound with precipices of crystalline snow; while a deep chasm drawn between the divide and the glacier separated the massive picture from everything else. Only the one sublime mountain in sight, the one glacier, and one lake; the whole veiled with one blue shadow—rock, ice and water, without a single leaf.

* * *

Descending the divide in a hesitating mood, I picked my way across the yawning chasm at the foot, and climbed out upon the glacier.

* * *

I could not distinctly hope to reach the summit from this side, yet I moved on across the glacier as if driven by fate. Contending with myself, the season is too far spent, I said, and even should I be successful, I might be storm-bound on the mountain; and in the cloud-darkness, with the cliffs and crevasses covered with snow, how could I escape? No. I must wait until next summer. I would only approach the mountain now, and inspect it, creep about its flanks, learn what I could of its history, holding myself ready to flee on the approach of the first storm-cloud. But we little know until tried how much of the uncontrollable there is in us, urging across glaciers and torrents, and up dangerous heights, let the judgment forbid as it may.

I succeeded in gaining the foot of the cliff on the eastern extremity of the glacier, and discovered the mouth of a narrow avalanche gully, through which I began to climb, intending to follow it as far as possible, and at least obtain some fine wild views for my pains. Its general course is oblique to the plane of the mountain-face, and the metamorphic slates of which it is built are cut by cleavage planes in such a way that they weather off in angular blocks, giving rise to irregular steps that greatly facilitate climbing on the sheer places. I thus made my way into a wilderness of crumbling spires and battlements, built together in bewildering combinations, and glazed in many places with a thin coating of ice, which I had to hammer off with a stone. The situation was becoming gradually more perilous; but, having passed several dangerous spots, I dared not think of descending; for, so steep was the entire ascent, one would inevitably fall to the glacier in case a single misstep were made. . . . At length, after attaining an elevation of 12,800 feet, I found myself at the foot of a sheer drop in the bed of the avalanche channel I was tracing, which seemed absolutely to bar all further progress. It is only about forty-five or fifty feet high, and somewhat roughened by fissures and projections; but these seemed so slight and insecure, as footholds, that I tried hard to avoid the precipice altogether, by scaling the wall on either side. But, though less steep, the walls were smoother than the obstructing rock, and repeated efforts only showed that I must either go right ahead or turn back. The tried dangers beneath seemed even greater than that of the cliff in front; therefore, after scanning its face again and again, I commenced to scale it, picking my holds with intense caution. After gaining a point about half-way to the top, I was suddenly brought to a dead stop, with arms outspread, clinging close to the face of the rock, unable to move hand or foot either up or down. My doom appeared fixed. I *must* fall. There would be a moment of bewilderment, and then a lifeless rumble down the one general precipice to the glacier below.

When this final danger flashed upon me, I became nerve-shaken for the first time since setting foot on the mountain, and my mind seemed to fill with a stifling smoke. But this terrible eclipse lasted only a moment, when life blazed forth again with preternatural clearness. I seemed suddenly to become possessed of a new sense. The other self—the ghost of by-gone experiences, Instinct, or Guardian Angel—call it what you will—came forward and assumed control. Then my trembling muscles became firm again, every rift and flaw in the rock was seen as through a microscope, and my limbs moved with a positiveness and precision with which I seemed to have nothing at all to do. Had I been borne aloft upon wings, my deliverance could not have been more complete.

Above this memorable spot, the face of the mountain is still more savagely hacked and torn. It is a maze of yawning chasms and gullies, in the angles of which rise beetling crags and piles of detached bowlders that seem to have been gotten ready to be launched below. But the strange influx of strength I had received seemed inexhaustible. I found a way without effort, and soon stood upon the topmost crag in the blessed light.

* * *

Looking southward along the axis of the range, the eye is first caught by a row of exceedingly sharp and slender spires, which rise openly to a height of about a thousand feet, from a series of short, residual glaciers that lean back against their bases; their fantastic sculpture and the unrelieved sharpness with which they spring out of the ice rendering them peculiarly wild and striking. These are "The Minarets," and beyond them you behold a most sublime wilderness of mountains, their snowy summits crowded together in lavish abundance, peak beyond peak, swelling higher, higher as they sweep on southward, until the culminating point of the range is reached on Mount Whitney, near the head of the Kern River, at an elevation of nearly 15,000 feet above the level of the sea.

Westward, the general flank of the range is seen flowing sublimely away from the sharp summits, in smooth undulations; a sea of gray granite waves dotted with lakes and meadows, and fluted with stupendous cañons that grow steadily deeper as they recede in the distance. Below this gray region lies the dark forest-zone, broken here and there by upswelling ridges and domes; and yet beyond is a yellow, hazy belt, marking the broad plain of the San Joaquin, bounded on its further side by the blue mountains of the coast. Turning now to the northward, there in the immediate foreground is the glorious Sierra Crown, with Cathedral Peak a few miles to the left—a temple of marvelous architecture, hewn from the living rock; the gray, giant form of Mammoth Mountain, 13,000 feet high; Mounts Ord, Gibbs, Dana, Conness, Tower Peak, Castle Peak, and Silver Mountain, stretching away in the distance, with a host of noble companions that are as yet nameless.

Eastward, the whole region seems a land of pure desolation covered with beautiful light. The torrid volcanic basin of Mono, with its one bare lake fourteen miles long; Owen's Valley and the broad lava table-land at its head, dotted with craters, and the massive Inyo Range, rivaling even the Sierra in height. These are spread, map-like, beneath you, with countless ranges beyond, passing and overlapping one another and fading on the glowing horizon.

* * *

But in the midst of these fine lessons and landscapes, I had to remember that the sun was wheeling far to the west, while a new way had to be discovered, at least to some point on the timber-line where I could have a fire; for I had not even burdened myself with a coat. I first scanned the western spurs, hoping some way might appear through which I might reach the northern glacier, and cross its snout; or pass around the lake into which it flows, and thus strike my morning track. This route was soon sufficiently unfolded to show that if practicable at all, it would require so much time that reaching camp that night would be out of the question. I therefore scrambled back eastward, descending the southern slopes obliquely at the same time. Here the crags seemed less formidable, and the head of a glacier that flows north-east came in sight, which I determined to follow as far as possible, hoping thus to make my way to the foot of the peak on the east side, and thence across the intervening cañons and ridges to camp.

The inclination of the glacier is quite moderate at the head, and, as the sun had softened the *névé*, I made safe and rapid progress, running and sliding, and keeping up a sharp outlook for crevasses. About half a mile from the head, there is an ice cascade, where the glacier pours over a sharp declivity, and is shattered into massive blocks separated by deep, blue fissures. . . . Fortunately, the day had been warm enough to loosen the ice-crystals so as to admit of hollows being dug in the rotten portions of the blocks, thus enabling me to pick my way with far less difficulty than I had anticipated.

* * *

Night drew near before I reached the eastern base of the mountain, and my camp lay many a rugged mile to the north; but ultimate success was assured. It was now only a matter of endurance and ordinary mountain-craft. The sunset was, if possible, yet more glorious than that of the day previous. The Mono landscape seemed to be fairly saturated with warm, purple light. The peaks marshaled along the summit were in shadow, but through every notch and pass streamed living sun-fire, soothing and irradiating their rough, black angles, while companies of small, luminous clouds hovered above them like very angels of light.

Darkness came on, but I found my way by the trends of the cañons and the peaks projected against the sky. All excitement died with the light, and then I was weary. But the joyful sound of the water-fall across the lake was heard at last, and soon the stars were seen reflected in the lake itself. Taking my bearings from these, I discovered the little pine thicket in which my nest was, and then I had a rest such as only a mountaineer may enjoy. Afterward, I made a sunrise fire, went down to the lake, dashed water on my head, and dipped a cupful for tea. The revival brought about by bread and tea was as complete as the exhaustion from excessive enjoyment and toil had been. Then I crept beneath the pine-tassels to bed. The wind was frosty and the fire burned low, but my sleep was none the less sound, and the evening constellations had swept far to the west before I awoke.

After warming and resting in the sunshine, I sauntered home,—that is, back to the Tuolumne camp,—bearing away toward a cluster of peaks that hold the fountain snows of one of the north tributaries of Rush Creek. Here I discovered a group of beautiful glacier lakes, nestled together in a grand amphitheater. Toward evening, I crossed the divide separating the Mono waters from those of the Tuolumne, and entered the glacier basin that now holds the fountain snows of the stream that forms the upper Tuolumne cascades. This stream I traced down through its many dells and gorges, meadows and bogs, reaching the brink of the main Tuolumne at dusk.

A loud whoop for the artists was answered again and again. Their camp-fire came in sight, and half an hour afterward I was with them.

They seemed unreasonably glad to see me. I had been absent only three days; nevertheless, they had already been weighing chances as to whether I would ever return, and trying to decide whether they should wait longer or begin to seek their way back to the lowlands. Now their curious troubles were over. They packed their precious sketches, and next morning we set out homeward bound, and in two days entered the Yosemite Valley from the north by way of Indian Cañon, and our fine double excursion was done.

Excerpted from "In the Heart of the California Alps," *Scribner's Monthly*, Vol. 20 No. 3, July 1880.

A Geologist's Winter Walk

In the winter of 1872, Muir spent two weeks in San Francisco, "terribly dazed and confused with the dust and din and heavy sticky air of that low region." Fleeing the lowlands, he returned to the Yosemite Valley in late December and decided to explore the full length of the Tenaya Canyon, which had never been done before. Muir's reaction to his fall on the canyon wall—his humorous address to his wayward feet and subsequent self-punishment—is reminiscent of his similar response when he nearly drowned as a boy at Fountain Lake. This event was first described in a letter to Muir's good friend, Mrs. Jeanne Carr.

AFTER REACHING TURLOCK, I sped afoot over the stubble fields and through miles of brown hemizonia and purple erigeron, to Hopeton, conscious of little more than that the town was behind and beneath me, and the mountains above and before me; on through the oaks and chaparral of the foothills to Coulterville; and then ascended the first great mountain step upon which grows the sugar pine. Here I slackened pace, for I drank the spicy, resiny wind, and beneath the arms of this noble tree I felt that I was safely home. Never did pine trees seem so dear. How sweet was their breath and their song, and how grandly they winnowed the sky!

I tingled my fingers among their tassels, and rustled my feet among their brown needles and burrs, and was exhilarated and joyful beyond all I can write.

When I reached Yosemite, all the rocks seemed talkative, and more telling and lovable than ever. They are dear friends, and seemed to have warm blood gushing through their granite flesh; and I love them with a love intensified by long and close companionship. After I had bathed in the bright river, sauntered over the meadows, conversed with the domes, and played with the pines, I still felt blurred and weary, as if tainted in some way with the sky of your streets. I determined, therefore, to run out for a while to say my prayers in the higher mountain temples. "The days are sunful," I said, "and, though now winter, no great danger need be encountered, and no sudden storm will block my return, if I am watchful."

The morning after this decision, I started up the cañon of Tenaya, caring little about the quantity of bread I carried; for, I thought, a fast and a storm and a difficult cañon were just the medicine I needed. When I passed Mirror Lake, I scarcely noticed it, for I was absorbed in the great Tissiack—her crown a mile away in the hushed azure; her purple granite drapery flowing in soft and graceful folds down to my feet, embroidered gloriously around with deep, shadowy forest. I have gazed on Tissiack a thousand times—in days of solemn storms, and when her form shone divine with the jewelry of winter, or when veiled in living clouds; and I have heard her voice of winds, and snowy, tuneful waters when floods were falling; yet never did her soul reveal itself more impressively than now. I hung about her skirts, lingering timidly, until the higher mountains and glaciers compelled me to push up the cañon.

This cañon is accessible only to mountaineers, and I was anxious to carry my barometer and clinometer through it, to obtain sections and altitudes, so I chose it as the most attractive highway. After I had passed the tall groves that stretch a mile above Mirror Lake, and scrambled around the Tenaya Fall, which is just at the head of the lake groves, I crept through the dense and spiny chaparral that plushes the roots of the mountains here for miles in warm green, and was ascending a precipitous rock-front, smoothed by glacial action, when I suddenly fell—for the first time since I touched foot to Sierra rocks. After several somersaults, I became insensible from the shock, and when consciousness returned I found myself wedged among short, stiff bushes, trembling as if cold, not injured in the slightest.

Judging by the sun, I could not have been insensible very long; probably not a minute, possibly an hour; and I could not remember what made me fall, or where I had fallen from; but I saw that if I had rolled a little further, my mountain-climbing would have been finished, for just beyond the bushes the cañon wall steepened and I might have fallen to the bottom. "There," said I, addressing my feet, to whose separate skill I had learned to trust night and day on any mountain, "that is what you get by intercourse with stupid town stairs, and dead pavements." I felt degraded and worthless. I had not yet reached the most difficult portion of the cañon, but I determined to guide my humbled body over the most nerve-trying places I could find; for I was now awake, and felt confident that the last of the town fog had been shaken from both head and feet.

I camped at the mouth of a narrow gorge which is cut into the bottom of the main cañon, determined to take earnest exercise next day. No plushy boughs did my ill-behaved bones enjoy that night, nor did my bumped head get a spicy cedar plume pillow mixed with flowers. I slept on a naked boulder, and when I awoke all my nervous trembling was gone.

The gorged portion of the cañon, in which I spent all the next day, is about a mile and a half in length; and I passed the time in tracing the action of the forces that determined this peculiar bottom gorge, which is an abrupt, ragged-walled, narrow-throated cañon, formed in the bottom of the wide-mouthed, smooth, and beveled main cañon. I will not stop now to tell you more; some day you may see it, like a shadowy line, from Cloud's Rest. In high water, the stream occupies all the bottom of the gorge, surging and chafing in glorious power from wall to wall. But the sound of the grinding was low as I entered the gorge, scarcely hoping to be able to pass through its entire length. By cool efforts, along glassy, ice-worn slopes, I reached the upper end in a little over a day, but was compelled to pass the second night in the gorge, and in the moonlight I wrote you this short pencil-letter in my notebook:—

> The moon is looking down into the cañon, and how marvelously the great rocks kindle to her light! Every dome, and brow, and swelling boss touched by her white rays, glows as if lighted with snow. I am now only a mile from last night's camp; and have been climbing and sketching all day in this difficult but instructive gorge. It is formed in the bottom of the main cañon, among the roots of Cloud's Rest. It begins at the filled-up lake-basin where I camped last night, and ends a few hundred yards above, in another basin of the same kind. The walls everywhere are craggy and vertical, and in some places

they overlean. It is only from twenty to sixty feet wide, and not, though black and broken enough, the thin, crooked mouth of some mysterious abyss; but it was eroded, for in many places I saw its solid, seamless floor.

I am sitting on a big stone, against which the stream divides, and goes brawling by in rapids on both sides; half of my rock is white in the light, half in shadow. As I look from the opening jaws of this shadowy gorge, South Dome is immediately in front—high in the stars, her face turned from the moon, with the rest of her body gloriously muffled in waved folds of granite. On the left, sculptured from the main Cloud's Rest ridge, are three magnificent rocks, sisters of the great South Dome. On the right is the massive, moonlit front of Mount Watkins, and between, low down in the furthest distance, is Sentinel Dome, girdled and darkened with forest. In the near foreground Tenaya Creek is singing against boulders that are white with snow and moonbeams. Now look back twenty yards, and you will see a waterfall fair as a spirit; the moonlight just touches it, bringing it into relief against a dark background of shadow. A little to the left, and a dozen steps this side of the fall, flickering light marks my camp—and a precious camp it is. A huge, glacier-polished slab, falling from the smooth, glossy flank of Cloud's Rest, happened to settle on edge against the wall of the gorge. I did not know that this slab was glacier-polished until I lighted my fire. Judge of my delight. I think it was sent here by an earthquake. It is about twelve feet square. I wish I could take it home for a hearthstone. Beneath this slab is the only place in this torrent-swept gorge where I could find sand sufficient for a bed.

I expected to sleep on the boulders, for I spent most of the afternoon on the slippery wall of the cañon, endeavoring to get around this difficult part of the gorge, and was compelled instead to hasten down here before dark. I shall sleep soundly on this sand; half of it is mica. Here, wonderful to behold, are a few green stems of prickly rubus, and a tiny grass. They are here to meet us. Ay, even here in this darksome gorge, "frightened and tormented" with raging torrents and choking avalanches of snow. Can it be? As if rubus and the grass leaf were not enough of God's tender prattle words of love, which we so much need in these mighty temples of power, yonder in the "benmost bore" are two blessed adiantums. Listen to them! How wholly infused with God is this one big word of love that we call the world! Good-night. Do you see the fire-glow on my ice-smoothed slab, and on my two ferns and the rubus and grass panicles? And do you hear how sweet a sleep song the fall and cascades are singing?

The water-ground chips and knots that I found fastened between the rocks kept my fire alive all through the night. Next morning I rose nerved and ready for another day of sketching and noting, and any form of climbing. I escaped from the gorge about noon, after accomplishing some of the most delicate feats of mountaineering I ever attempted; and here the cañon is all broadly open again—the floor luxuriantly forested with pine, and spruce, and silver fir, and brown-trunked libocedrus. The walls rise in Yosemite forms, and Tenaya Creek comes down seven hundred feet in a white brush of foam. This is a little Yosemite valley. It is about two thousand feet above the level of the main Yosemite, and about twenty-four hundred below Lake Tenaya.

I found the lake frozen, and the ice was so clear and unruffled that the surrounding mountains and the groves that look down upon it were reflected almost as perfectly as I ever beheld them in the calm evening mirrors of summer. At a little distance, it was difficult to believe the lake frozen at all; and when I walked out on it, cautiously stamping at short intervals to test the strength of the ice, I seemed to walk mysteriously, without adequate faith, on the surface of the water. The ice was so transparent that I could see through it the beautifully wave-rippled, sandy bottom, and the scales of mica glinting back the down-pouring light. When I knelt down with my face close to the ice, through which the sunbeams were pouring, I was delighted to discover myriads of Tyndall's six-rayed water flowers, magnificently colored.

A grand old mountain mansion is this Tenaya region! In the glacier period it was a *mer de glace*, far grander than the *mer de glace* of Switzerland, which is only about half a mile broad. The Tenaya *mer de glace* was not less than two miles broad, late in the glacier epoch, when all the principal dividing crests were bare; and its depth was not less than fifteen hundred feet. Ice-streams from Mounts Lyell and Dana, and all the mountains between, and from the nearer Cathedral Peak, flowed hither, welded into one, and worked together. After eroding this Tenaya Lake basin, and all the splendidly sculptured rocks and mountains that surround and adorn it, and the great Tenaya Cañon, with its wealth of all that makes mountains sublime, they were welded with the vast South, Lyell, and

Illilouette glaciers on one side, and with those of Hoffman on the other—thus forming a portion of a yet grander *mer de glace* in Yosemite Valley.

I reached the Tenaya Cañon, on my way home, by coming in from the northeast, rambling down over the shoulders of Mount Watkins, touching bottom a mile above Mirror Lake. From thence home was but a saunter in the moonlight.

After resting one day, and the weather continuing calm, I ran up over the left shoulder of South Dome and down in front of its grand split face to make some measurements, completed my work, climbed to the right shoulder, struck off along the ridge for Cloud's Rest, and reached the topmost heave of her sunny wave in ample time to see the sunset.

Cloud's Rest is a thousand feet higher than Tissiack. It is a wavelike crest upon a ridge, which begins at Yosemite with Tissiack, and runs continuously eastward to the thicket of peaks and crests around Lake Tenaya. This lofty granite wall is bent this way and that by the restless and weariless action of glaciers just as if it had been made of dough. But the grand circumference of mountains and forests are coming from far and near, densing into one close assemblage; for the sun, their god and father, with love ineffable, is glowing a sunset farewell. Not one of all the assembled rocks or trees seemed remote. How impressively their faces shone with responsive love!

I ran home in the moonlight with firm strides; for the sun-love made me strong. Down through the junipers; down through the firs; now in jet shadows, now in white light; over sandy moraines and bare, clanking rocks; past the huge ghost of South Dome rising weird through the firs; past the glorious fall of Nevada, the groves of Illilouette; through the pines of the valley; beneath the bright crystal sky blazing with stars. All of this mountain wealth in one day!—one of the rich ripe days that enlarge one's life; so much of the sun upon one side of it, so much of the moon and stars on the other.

Excerpted from *Steep Trails*, edited by William Frederic Badè. Boston and New York: Houghton Mifflin Company, 1918.

The Tree Ride

This fine essay that Muir called "Wind-storm in the Forests of the Yuba" describes an incident that occurred in 1874. First published in Scribner's Monthly *and reprinted many times, it represents the first time that Muir consciously chose to make himself the subject of his writing. For many Americans, this account of a thrilling tree ride in the wind was a memorable introduction to Muir's spirit and acute powers of observation. His immense popularity as a nature writer for the major magazines of his day was well established by the late 1870s. Muir called the tree he climbed a Douglas Spruce—it is now known as the Douglas Fir.*

ONE OF THE MOST BEAUTIFUL AND EXHILARATING STORMS I ever enjoyed in the Sierra occurred in December, 1874, when I happened to be exploring one of the tributary valleys of the Yuba River. The sky and the ground and the trees had been thoroughly rain-washed and was dry again. The day was intensely pure, one of those incomparable bits of California winter, warm and balmy and full of white sparkling sunshine, redolent of all the purest influences of the spring, and at the same time enlivened with one of the most bracing wind-storms conceivable. Instead of camping out, as I usually do, I then chanced to be stopping at the house of a friend. But when the storm began to sound, I lost no time in pushing out into the woods to enjoy it. For on such occasions Nature has always something rare to show us, and the danger to life and limb is hardly greater than one would experience crouching deprecatingly beneath a roof.

It was still early morning when I found myself fairly adrift. Delicious sunshine came pouring over the hills, lighting the tops of the pines, and setting free a steam of summery fragrance that contrasted strangely with the wild tones of the storm. The air was mottled with pine-tassels and bright green plumes, that went flashing past in the sunlight like birds pursued. But there was not the slightest dustiness, nothing less pure than leaves, and ripe pollen, and flecks of withered bracken and moss. I heard trees falling for hours at the rate of one every two or three minutes; some uprooted, partly on account of the loose, water-soaked condition of the ground; others broken straight across, where some weakness caused by fire had determined the spot. The gestures of the various trees made a delightful study. Young Sugar Pines, light and feathery as squirrel-tails, were bowing almost to the ground; while the grand old patriarchs, whose massive boles had been tried in a hundred storms, waved solemnly above them, their long, arching branches streaming fluently on the gale, and every needle thrilling and ringing and shedding off keen lances of light like a diamond. The Douglas Spruces, with long sprays drawn out in level tresses, and needles massed in a gray, shimmering glow, presented a most striking appearance as they stood in bold relief along the hilltops. The madroños in the dells, with their red bark and large glossy leaves tilted every way, reflected the sunshine in throbbing spangles like those one so often sees on the rippled surface of a glacier lake. But the Silver Pines were now the most impressively beautiful of all. Colossal spires 200 feet in height waved like supple goldenrods chanting and bowing low as if in worship, while the whole mass of their long, tremulous foliage was kindled into one continuous blaze of white sun-fire. The force of the gale was such that the most steadfast monarch of them all rocked down to its roots with a motion plainly perceptible when one leaned against it. Nature was holding high festival, and every fiber of the most rigid giants thrilled with glad excitement.

I drifted on through the midst of this passionate music and motion, across many a glen, from ridge to ridge; often halting in the lee of a rock for shelter, or to gaze and listen. Even when the grand anthem had swelled to its highest pitch, I could distinctly hear the varying tones of individual trees,—Spruce, and Fir, and Pine, and leafless Oak,—and even the infinitely gentle rustle of the withered grasses at my feet. Each was expressing itself in its own way,—singing its own song, and making its own peculiar gestures,—manifesting a richness of variety to be found in no other forest I have yet seen. The coniferous woods of Canada, and the Carolinas, and Florida, are made up of trees that resemble one another about as nearly as blades of grass, and grow close together in much the same way. Coniferous trees, in general, seldom possess individual character, such as is manifest among Oaks and Elms. But the California forests are made up of a greater number of distinct species than any other in the world. And in them we find, not only a marked differentiation into special groups, but also a marked individuality in almost every tree, giving rise to storm effects indescribably glorious.

Toward midday, after a long, tingling scramble through copses of hazel and ceanothus, I gained the summit of the highest ridge in the neighborhood; and then it occurred to me that it would be a fine thing to climb one of the trees to obtain a wider outlook and get my ear close to the Æolian music of its topmost needles. But under the circumstances the choice of a tree was a serious matter. One whose instep was not very strong seemed in danger of being blown down, or of being struck by others in case they should fall; another was branchless to a considerable height above the ground, and at the same time too large to be grasped with arms and legs in climbing; while others were not favorably situated for clear views. After cautiously casting about, I made a choice of the tallest of a group of Douglas Spruces that were growing close together like a tuft of grass, no one of which seemed likely to fall unless all the rest fell with it. Though comparatively young, they were about 100 feet high, and their lithe, brushy tops were rocking and swirling in wild ecstasy. Being accustomed to climb trees in making botanical studies, I experienced no difficulty in reaching the top of this one, and never before did I enjoy so noble an exhilaration of motion. The slender tops fairly flapped and swished in the passionate torrent, bending and swirling backward and forward, round and round, tracing indescribable combinations of vertical and horizontal curves, while I clung with muscles firm braced, like a bobolink on a reed.

In its widest sweeps my tree-top described an arc of from twenty to thirty degrees, but I felt sure of its elastic temper, having seen others of the same species still more severely tried—bent almost to the ground indeed, in heavy snows—without breaking a fiber. I was therefore safe, and free to take the wind into my pulses and enjoy the excited forest from my superb outlook. The view from here must be extremely beautiful in any weather. Now my eye roved over the piny hills and dales as over fields of waving grain, and felt the light running in ripples and broad swelling undulations across the valleys from ridge to ridge, as the shining foliage was stirred by corresponding waves of air. Oftentimes these waves of reflected light would break up suddenly into a kind of beaten foam, and again, after chasing one another in regular order, they would seem to bend forward in concentric curves, and disappear on some hillside, like sea-waves on a shelving shore. The quantity of light reflected from the bent needles was so great as to make whole groves appear as if covered with snow, while the black shadows beneath the trees greatly enhanced the effect of the silvery splendor.

Excepting only the shadows there was nothing somber in all this wild sea of pines. On the contrary, notwithstanding this was the winter season, the colors were remarkably beautiful. The shafts of the pine and libocedrus were brown and purple, and most of the foliage was well tinged with yellow; the laurel groves, with the pale undersides of their leaves turned upward, made masses of gray; and then there was many a dash of chocolate color from clumps of manzanita, and jet of vivid crimson from the bark of the madroños, while the ground on the hillsides, appearing here and there through openings between the groves, displayed masses of pale purple and brown.

The sounds of the storm corresponded gloriously with this wild exuberance of light and motion. The profound bass of the naked branches and boles booming like waterfalls; the quick, tense vibrations of the pine-needles, now rising to a shrill, whistling hiss, now falling to a silky murmur; the rustling of laurel groves in the dells, and the keen metallic click of leaf on leaf—all this was heard in easy analysis when the attention was calmly bent.

The varied gestures of the multitude were seen to fine advantage, so that one could recognize the different species at a distance of several miles by this means alone, as well as by their forms and colors, and the way they reflected the light. All seemed strong and comfortable, as if really enjoying the storm, while responding to its most enthusiastic greetings. We hear much nowadays concerning the universal struggle for existence, but no struggle in the common meaning of the word was manifest here; no recognition of danger by any tree; no deprecation; but rather an invincible gladness as remote from exultation as from fear.

I kept my lofty perch for hours, frequently closing my eyes to enjoy the music by itself, or to feast quietly on the delicious fragrance that was streaming past. The fragrance of the woods was less marked than that produced during warm rain, when so many balsamic buds and leaves are steeped like tea; but, from the chafing of resiny branches against each other, and the incessant attrition of myriads of needles, the gale was spiced to a very tonic degree. And besides the fragrance from these local sources there were traces of scents brought from afar. For this wind came first from the sea, rubbing against its fresh, briny waves, then distilled through the redwoods, threading rich ferny gulches, and spreading itself in broad undulating currents over many a flower-enameled ridge of the coast mountains, then across the golden plains, up the purple foot-hills, and into these piny woods with the varied incense gathered by the way.

Winds are advertisements of all they touch, however much or little we may be able to read them; telling their wanderings even by their scents alone. Mariners detect the flowery perfume of land-winds far at sea, and sea-winds carry the fragrance of dulse and tangle far inland, where it is quickly recognized, though mingled with the scents of a thousand land-flowers. As an illustration of this, I may tell here that I breathed sea-air on the Firth of Forth, in Scotland, while a boy; then was taken to Wisconsin, where I remained nineteen years; then, without in all this time having breathed one breath of the sea, I walked quietly, alone, from the middle of the Mississippi Valley to the Gulf of Mexico, on a botanical excursion, and while in Florida, far from the coast, my attention wholly bent on the splendid tropical vegetation about me, I suddenly recognized a sea-breeze, as it came sifting through the palmettos and blooming vine-tangles, which at once awakened and set free a thousand dormant associations, and made me a boy again in Scotland, as if all the intervening years had been annihilated.

Most people like to look at mountain rivers, and bear them in mind; but few care to look at the winds, though far more beautiful and sublime, and though they become at times about as visible as flowing water. When the north winds in winter are making upward sweeps over the curving summits of the High Sierra, the fact is sometimes published with flying snow-banners a mile long. Those portions of the winds thus embodied can scarce be wholly invisible, even to the darkest imagination. And when we look around over an agitated forest, we may see something of the wind that stirs it, by its effects upon the trees. Yonder it descends in a rush of water-like ripples, and sweeps over the bending pines from hill to hill. Nearer, we see detached plumes and leaves, now speeding by on level currents, now whirling in eddies, or, escaping over the edges of the whirls, soaring aloft on grand, upswelling domes of air, or tossing on flame-like crests. Smooth, deep currents, cascades, falls, and swirling eddies, sing around every tree and leaf, and over all the varied topography of the region with telling changes of form, like mountain rivers conforming to the features of their channels.

After tracing the Sierra streams from their fountains to the plains, marking where they bloom white in falls, glide in crystal plumes, surge gray and foam-filled in boulder-choked gorges, and slip through the woods in long, tranquil reaches—after thus learning their language and forms in detail, we may at length hear them chanting all together in one grand anthem, and comprehend them all in clear inner vision, covering the range like lace. But even this spectacle is far less sublime and not a whit more substantial than what we may behold of these storm-streams of air in the mountain woods.

We all travel the milky way together, trees and men; but it never occurred to me until this storm-day, while swinging in the wind, that trees are travelers, in the ordinary sense. They make many journeys, not extensive ones, it is true; but our own little journeys, away and back again, are only little more than tree-wavings—many of them not so much.

When the storm began to abate, I dismounted and sauntered down through the calming woods. The storm-tones died away, and, turning toward the east, I beheld the countless hosts of the forests hushed and tranquil, towering above one another on the slopes of the hills like a devout audience. The setting sun filled them with amber light, and seemed to say, while they listened, "My peace I give unto you."

As I gazed on the impressive scene, all the so-called ruin of the storm was forgotten, and never before did these noble woods appear so fresh, so joyous, so immortal.

Excerpted from *The Mountains of California*. New York: The Century Co., 1894.

A Perilous Night on Mount Shasta

In 1875, after only a half dozen years of mountaineering, Muir's confidence in his abilities could not be better demonstrated than in his several ascents of the 14,142 foot Mount Shasta. On this particular "perilous night," in the midst of his agonizing discomfort, it's striking that he found himself contemplating the beauty of the stars as the storm cleared. The "frost-nipping" suffered on his feet resulted in a slight limp noticeable in his old age.

On the 28th of April [1875] I led a party up the mountain for the purpose of making a survey of the summit with reference to the location of the Geodetic monument. On the 30th, accompanied by Jerome Fay, I made another ascent to make some barometrical observations, the day intervening between the two ascents being devoted to establishing a camp on the extreme edge of the timber-line. Here, on our red trachyte bed, we obtained two hours of shallow sleep broken for occasional glimpses of the keen, starry night. At two o'clock we rose, breakfasted on a warmed tin-cupful of coffee and a piece of frozen venison broiled on the coals, and started for the summit. Up to this time there was nothing in sight that betokened the approach of a storm; but on gaining the summit, we saw toward Lassen's Butte hundreds of square miles of white cumuli boiling dreamily in the sunshine far beneath us, and causing no alarm.

The slight weariness of the ascent was soon rested away, and our glorious morning in the sky promised nothing but enjoyment. At 9 A.M. the dry thermometer stood at 34° in the shade and rose steadily until at 1 P.M. it stood at 50°, probably influenced somewhat by radiation from the sun-warmed cliffs. A common bumble-bee, not at all benumbed, zigzagged vigorously about our heads for a few moments, as if unconscious of the fact that the nearest honey flower was a mile beneath him.

In the mean time clouds were growing down in Shasta Valley—massive swelling cumuli, displaying delicious tones of purple and gray in the hollows of their sun-beaten bosses. Extending gradually southward around on both sides of Shasta, these at length united with the older field towards Shasta's Butte, thus encircling Mount Shasta in one continuous cloud-zone. Rhett and Klamath Lakes were eclipsed beneath clouds scarcely less brilliant than their own silvery disks. The Modoc Lava Beds, many a snow-laden peak far north in Oregon, the Scott and Trinity and Siskiyou Mountains, the peaks of the Sierra, the blue Coast Range, Shasta Valley, the dark forests filling the valley of the Sacramento, all in turn were obscured or buried, leaving the lofty cone on which we stood solitary in the sunshine between two skies—a sky of spotless blue above, a sky of glittering cloud beneath. The creative sun shone glorious on the vast expanse of cloudland; hill and dale, mountain and valley springing into existence responsive to his rays and steadily developing in beauty and individuality. One huge mountain-cone of cloud, corresponding to Mount Shasta in these newborn cloud-ranges, rose close alongside with a visible motion, its firm, polished bosses soaring so near and substantial that we almost fancied we might leap down upon them from where we stood and make our way to the lowlands. No hint was given, by anything in their appearance, of the fleeting character of these most sublime and beautiful cloud mountains. On the contrary they impressed one as being lasting additions to the landscape.

The weather of the springtime and summer, throughout the Sierra in general, is usually varied by slight local rains and dustings of snow, most of which are obviously far too joyous and life-giving to be regarded as storms—single clouds growing in the sunny sky, ripening in an hour, showering the heated landscape, and passing away like a thought, leaving no visible bodily remains to stain the sky. Snowstorms of the same gentle kind abound among the high peaks, but in spring they not unfrequently attain larger proportions, assuming a violence and energy of expression scarcely surpassed by those bred in the depths of winter. Such was the storm now gathering about us.

It began to declare itself shortly after noon, suggesting to us the idea of at once seeking our safe camp in the timber and abandoning the purpose of making an observation of the barometer at 3 P.M.,—two having already been made, at 9 A.M., and 12 M., while simultaneous observations were made at Strawberry Valley. Jerome peered at short intervals over the ridge, contemplating the rising clouds with anxious gestures in the rough wind, and at length declared that if we did not make a speedy escape we should be compelled to pass the rest of the day and night on the summit. But anxiety to complete my observations stifled my own instinctive promptings to retreat, and held me to my work. No inexperienced person was depending on me, and I told Jerome that we two mountaineers should be able to make our way down through any storm likely to fall.

Presently thin, fibrous films of cloud began to blow directly over the summit from north to south, drawn out in long fairy webs like carded wool, forming and dissolving as if by magic. The wind twisted them into ringlets and whirled them in a succession of graceful convolutions like the outside sprays of Yosemite Falls in flood-time; then, sailing out into the thin azure over the precipitous brink of the ridge they were drifted together like wreaths of foam on a river. These higher and finer cloud fabrics were evidently produced by the chilling of the air from its own expansion caused by the upward deflection of the wind against the slopes of the mountain. They steadily increased on the north rim of the cone, forming at length a thick, opaque, ill-defined embankment from the icy meshes of which snowflowers began to fall, alternating with hail. The sky speedily darkened, and just as I had completed my last observation and boxed my instruments ready for the descent, the storm began in serious earnest. At first the cliffs were beaten with hail, every stone of which, as far as I could see, was regular in form, six-sided pyramids with rounded base, rich and sumptuous-looking, and fashioned with loving care, yet seemingly thrown away on those desolate crags down which they went rolling, falling, sliding in a network of curious streams.

After we had forced our way down the ridge and past the group of hissing fumaroles, the storm became inconceivably violent. The thermometer fell 22° in a few minutes, and soon dropped below zero. The hail gave place to snow, and darkness came on like night. The wind, rising to the highest pitch of violence, boomed and surged amid the desolate crags;

lightning-flashes in quick succession cut the gloomy darkness; and the thunders, the most tremendously loud and appalling I ever heard, made an almost continuous roar, stroke following stroke in quick, passionate succession, as though the mountain were being rent to its foundations and the fires of the old volcano were breaking forth again.

Could we at once have begun to descend the snow-slopes leading to the timber, we might have made good our escape, however dark and wild the storm. As it was, we had first to make our way along a dangerous ridge nearly a mile and a half long, flanked in many places by steep ice-slopes at the head of the Whitney Glacier on one side and by shattered precipices on the other. Apprehensive of this coming darkness, I had taken the precaution, when the storm began, to make the most dangerous points clear to my mind, and to mark their relations with reference to the direction of the wind. When, therefore, the darkness came on, and the bewildering drift, I felt confident that we could force our way through it with no other guidance. After passing the "Hot Springs" I halted in the lee of a lava-block to let Jerome, who had fallen a little behind, come up. Here he opened a council in which, under circumstances sufficiently exciting but without evincing any bewilderment, he maintained, in opposition to my views, that it was impossible to proceed. He firmly refused to make the venture to find the camp, while I, aware of the dangers that would necessarily attend our efforts, and conscious of being the cause of his present peril, decided not to leave him.

Our discussions ended, Jerome made a dash from the shelter of the lava-block and began forcing his way back against the wind to the "Hot Springs," wavering and struggling to resist being carried away, as if he were fording a rapid stream. After waiting and watching in vain for some flaw in the storm that might be urged as a new argument in favor of attempting the descent, I was compelled to follow. "Here," said Jerome, as we shivered in the midst of the hissing, sputtering fumaroles, "we shall be safe from frost." "Yes," said I, "we can lie in this mud and steam and sludge, warm at least on one side; but how can we protect our lungs from the acid gases, and how, after our clothing is saturated, shall we be able to reach camp without freezing, even after the storm is over? We shall have to wait for sunshine, and when will it come?"

The tempered area to which we had committed ourselves extended over about one fourth of an acre; but it was only about an eighth of an inch in thickness, for the scalding gas-jets were shorn off close to the ground by the oversweeping flood of frosty wind. And how lavishly the snow fell only mountaineers may know. The crisp crystal flowers seemed to touch one another and fairly to thicken the tremendous blast that carried them. This was the bloom-time, the summer of the cloud, and never before have I seen even a mountain cloud flowering so profusely.

When the bloom of the Shasta chaparral is falling, the ground is sometimes covered for hundreds of square miles to a depth of half an inch. But the bloom of this fertile snow-cloud grew and matured and fell to a depth of two feet in a few hours. Some crystals landed with their rays almost perfect, but most of them were worn and broken by striking against one another, or by rolling on the ground. The touch of these snow-flowers in calm weather is infinitely gentle—glinting, swaying, settling silently in the dry mountain air, or massed in flakes soft and downy. To lie out alone in the mountains of a still night and be touched by the first of these small silent messengers from the sky is a memorable experience, and the fineness of that touch none will forget. But the storm-blast laden with crisp, sharp snow seems to crush and bruise and stupefy with its multitude of stings, and compels the bravest to turn and flee.

The snow fell without abatement until an hour or two after what seemed to be the natural darkness of the night. Up to the time the storm first broke on the summit its development was remarkably gentle. There was a deliberate growth of clouds, a weaving of translucent tissue above, then the roar of the wind and the thunder, and the darkening flight of snow. Its subsidence was not less sudden. The clouds broke and vanished, not a crystal was left in the sky, and the stars shone out with pure and tranquil radiance.

During the storm we lay on our backs so as to present as little surface as possible to the wind, and to let the drift pass over us. The mealy snow sifted into the folds of our clothing and in many places reached the skin. We were glad at first to see the snow packing about us, hoping it would deaden the force of the wind, but it soon froze into a stiff, crusty heap as the temperature fell, rather augmenting our novel misery.

When the heat became unendurable, on some spot where steam was escaping through the sludge, we tried to stop it with snow and mud, or shifted a little at a time by shoving with our heels; for to stand in blank exposure to the fearful wind in our frozen-and-broiled condition seemed certain death. The acrid incrustations sublimed from the escaping gases frequently gave way, opening new vents to scald us; and, fearing that if at any time the wind should fall, carbonic acid, which often formed a considerable portion of the gaseous exhalations of volcanoes, might collect insufficient quantities to cause sleep and death, I warned Jerome against forgetting himself for a single moment, even should his sufferings admit of such a thing.

Accordingly, when during the long, dreary watches of the night we roused from a state of half-consciousness, we called each other by name in a frightened, startled way, each fearing the other might be benumbed or dead. The ordinary sensations of cold give but a faint conception of that which comes on after hard climbing with want of food and sleep in such exposure as this. Life is then seen to be a fire, that now smoulders, now brightens, and may be easily quenched. The weary hours wore away like dim half-forgotten years, so long and eventful they seemed, though we did nothing but suffer. Still the pain was not always of that bitter, intense kind that precludes thought and takes away all capacity for enjoyment. A sort of dreamy stupor came on at times in which we fancied we saw dry, resinous logs suitable for campfires, just as after going days without food men fancy they see bread.

Frozen, blistered, famished, benumbed, our bodies seemed lost to us at times—all dead but the eyes. For the duller and fainter we became the clearer was our vision, though only in momentary glimpses. Then, after the sky cleared, we gazed at the stars, blessed immortals of light, shining with marvelous brightness with long lance rays, near-looking and new-looking, as if never seen before. Again they would look familiar and remind us of stargazing at home. Oftentimes imagination coming into play would present charming pictures of the warm zone below, mingled with others near and far. Then the bitter wind and the drift would break the blissful vision and dreary pains cover us like clouds. "Are you suffering much?" Jerome would inquire with pitiful faintness. "Yes," I would say, striving to keep my voice brave, "frozen and burned; but never mind, Jerome, the night will wear away at last, and to-morrow we go a-Maying, and what campfires we will make, and what sunbaths we will take!"

The frost grew more and more intense, and we became icy and covered over with a crust of frozen snow, as if we had lain cast away in the drift all winter. In about thirteen hours—every hour like a year—day began to dawn, but it was long ere the summit's rocks were touched by the sun. No clouds were visible from where we lay, yet the morning was dull and blue, and bitterly frosty; and hour after hour passed by while we eagerly watched the pale light stealing down the ridge to the hollow where we lay. But there was not a trace of that warm, flushing sunrise splendor we so long had hoped for.

As the time drew near to make an effort to reach camp, we became concerned to know what strength was left us, and whether or no we could walk; for we had lain flat all this time without once rising to our feet. Mountaineers, however, always find in themselves a reserve of power after great exhaustion. It is a kind of second life, available only in emergencies like this; and, having proved its existence, I had no great fear that either of us would fail, though one of my arms was already benumbed and hung powerless.

At length, after the temperature was somewhat mitigated on this memorable first of May, we arose and began to struggle homeward. Our frozen trousers could scarcely be made to bend at the knee, and we waded the snow with difficulty. The summit ridge was fortunately wind-swept and nearly bare, so we were not compelled to lift our feet high, and on reaching the long home slopes laden with loose snow we made rapid progress, sliding and shuffling and pitching headlong, our feebleness accelerating rather than diminishing our speed. When we had descended some three thousand feet the sunshine warmed our backs and we began to revive. At 10 A.M. we reached the timber and were safe.

Half an hour later we heard Sisson shouting down among the firs, coming with horses to take us to the hotel. After breaking a trail through the snow as far as possible he had tied his animals and walked up. We had been so long without food that we cared but little about eating, but we eagerly drank the coffee he prepared for us. Our feet were frozen, and thawing them was painful, and had to be done very slowly by keeping them buried in soft snow for several hours, which avoided permanent-damage. Five thousand feet below the summit we found only three inches of new snow, and at the base of the mountain only a slight shower of rain had fallen, showing how local our storm had been, notwithstanding its terrific fury. Our feet were wrapped in sacking, and we were soon mounted and on our way down into the thick sunshine—"God's Country," as Sisson calls the Chaparral Zone. In two hours' ride the last snow-bank was left behind. Violets appeared along the edges of the trail, and the chaparral was coming into bloom, with young lilies and larkspurs about the open places in rich profusion. How beautiful seemed the golden sunbeams streaming through the woods between the warm brown boles of the cedars and pines! All my friends among the birds and plants seemed like old friends, and we felt like speaking to every one of them as we passed, as if we had been a long time away in some far, strange country.

In the afternoon we reached Strawberry Valley and fell asleep. Next morning we seemed to have risen from the dead. My bedroom was flooded with sunshine, and from the window I saw the great white Shasta cone clad in forests and clouds and bearing them loftily in the sky. Everything seemed full and radiant with the freshness and beauty and enthusiasm of youth. Sisson's children came in with flowers and covered my bed, and the storm on the mountaintop vanished like a dream.

Excerpted from *Steep Trails*, edited by William Frederic Badè. Boston and New York: Houghton Mifflin Company, 1918.

An independent account of Muir's trial on Mount Shasta is provided by the following report. It was written by Augustus Frederick Rodgers, who had hired Muir and Fay for the ascent, addressed to the Superintendent of the United States Coast Survey, C. P. Patterson, and dated the 8th of May, 1875. Note that while Muir wrote of misery enough in his own account, he did not mention that he had no coat at the summit, nor that his beard had frozen to his box of instruments. The summit register of 1875, now at the Bancroft Library at the University of California at Berkeley, shows that Muir and Fay made the ascent from timberline—a gain in elevation of about 7,000 feet—in four hours and ten minutes.

REPORT TO THE SUPERINTENDENT
by Augustus Frederick Rodgers

April 30th

Mr. Muir & Fay the guide are to make an early start from the higher camp ground & signal me from Shasta's snowy peak by 9 A.M. with mirror, as evidence of observing barometer simultaneously with me—8.45 A.M. flashes from the mountain answered by me from the valley—excite the Siskiyou barbarians & back woodsmen & notify me of Mr. Muir being good to his work & on time—Barometers observed Muir No 1544—I 1571—same at 12 M. at 1 P.M. portentous clouds cover the sky & at 2 P.M. quite a heavy thunder shower in Strawberry Valley, The clouds shutting out Shasta's Peak—hope Muir will not attempt to wait for the 3 o'clock observation of barometer.—Rain all the afternoon & towards sundown partially clears—can see that snow has whitened Shasta since morning—looked for the upper camp fire, which was plainly visible last night, as an evidence of Muir & Fay having safely gottened down the mountain—no signal fire in sight and conclude they have come down to the lower camp for better shelter, & are out of sight from the valley.

May 1st

Sisson left at 5 A.M. to break camp on Shasta's flank & bring down camp traps with Mr Muir & Fay, left early enough to get Mr Muir down in time to leave with me in stage at 4 P.M. this afternoon for Redding, en route to San Francisco—Sisson expected to be back at 1 P.M. but 4 P.M. passed & no news of the party, the natives commenced to gather in front of Sisson's House & say "something is wrong with them fellows," an apprehension which I must say I did not share knowing them both to be experienced mountaineers; about 5 P.M. Sisson came in sight with two very weather beaten men, hardly recognizable Muir in his stocking feet & Fay walking with considerable difficulty from the horse block to the house—Muir insisted on staying for the 3 o'clock observation & observed it in a storm of snow & hail so blinding that it was considered more risky to attempt to get down to camp than to stay on the summit and take the chances of freezing—2 ft of snow fell on the summit & Muir & Fay kept themselves alive in the intense cold, the former without a coat of any kind, by lying down on the hot spring ground—actually scalding the skin off of back &

hips in blisters where ever the contact was too close, Mr. Muir regretted that he could not answer my inquiry as to the degree of cold.—by saying that "while his back was scalding his beard & watch chain & two Barometer guards were all frozen together & he had not the courage to go ten feet off to get the Thermometer cases" although he knew it would be a matter of interest to observe them. At 8 o'clock this morning Mr Muir & Fay made up their minds to break out from the summit & get to camp—after leaving the hot springs every stitch of clothing was frozen stiff upon them & in crossing the snow field their feet became frosted in spite of every precaution one of Fay's feet is badly frosted & both of Muir severely touched—bathe the feet in ice cold water, apply bandages to the feet & one of the natives has a balm for the hot spring blisters—which he proceeds to apply. Hang Cistern Barometer No 1544 taken to the summit by Muir & compare it with 1571 taken up by me—comparisons good—Muir's observations and mine at the summit agree.

May 2d

Muir & Fay both look as if they had been on a "terrible tear" eyes bloodshot, faces red & swollen & altogether two very disreputable persons—Mr. Muir although lying in bed with his stocking feet constantly wet & exposed to the air, thinks he will be able to take the stage this afternoon.

Mono Lake Windstorm

This incident, found in Muir's journal, probably took place in the summer of 1875. It is likely that the three companions were educators John Swett and J. B. McChesney, and the artist William Keith, all of whom became cherished friends of Muir.

Mono Lake is well-known for its sudden tempests. Muir was a seasoned wilderness wanderer, but the pleas of his discomforted fellow travelers seem to have clouded his judgment.

Mono Lake
June 20.

A windstorm.

THE PARTY OF THREE THAT I LED THROUGH THE PASS to Mono Lake, were eager to sail its heavy waters and visit the islands. We borrowed an old waterlogged boat from a nomad who was stopping there for a while. He cautioned us against delaying our return, as stormy winds often raised a heavy sea. . . . The lake was calm, lying like a sheet of molten metal—a dead lake in every sense. We paddled gently, rambling along the white shore curves, careful not to overbalance the clumsy craft that seemed trying to turn turtle.

A sail on the lake develops a group of pictures of rare beauty and grandeur. Long, ranks of snowy swans on the dark water, clouds of ducks enveloped in silvery spangles. The mighty barren Sierra rising abruptly from the waters to a height of seven thousand feet, and stretching north and south for twenty miles with rows of snowy peaks. Ranges of cumulus clouds swelling in massive bosses of pearl—cloud-mountains and rock-mountains equally grand and substantial in appearance. Snowfields and ice in the higher hollows, white torrents dashing down shadowy groves, and smooth moraine slopes drawn out upon the gray sage plains along the base of the range, with silvery streams descending in bright cheery song to vanish in the dry desert.

The larger island in the lake is about two and a half miles long, and is composed of hard lava and loose ashes. The smaller, half a mile long with a cone two hundred and forty feet high, is of hard black lava, quite recent. Boiling springs and hot jets of gas boil up from the lake-bottom near its shore. . . .

In two hours we gained the larger island and wandered about looking at the cone basalt, lavas, hot springs, and vegetation. . . . A few white and blue gulls slowly winnowed the air on the way to their homes, while here and there the swift wing of a swallow was seen. . . .

Then clouds began to settle low on the dark cluster of peaks about Mount Ritter and at the head of Rush Creek, allowing the hacked summits to appear free above them. Mount Dana had a round gray cloud-cap which at first lightly touched, then gently clasped his snowy head. Heavy cumuli gathered and grew to the northeastward toward Aurora, and shadows crept across the gray levels about the lake.

Suddenly, at noon, a breeze fell from the mountains which soon roused the sleeping waters into white-crested waves. . . .

Then we made haste to get back to the mainland, a distance of about seven miles from the island. After rowing hard and going about a third of the way, the wind began to blow in heavy surges that lashed the lake into a fierce roaring tempest. Water poured over the boat, faster than we could bail it out. Fearing we should sink, we turned back to the island, glad to get ashore anywhere. The waves broke unweariedly on the sloping beach, waking memories of my boyhood on the seashore of Scotland. . . . I advised waiting patiently until the next day, but my comrades, hungry and without blankets, began to murmur. However, they submitted and went to bed, but the fire of slight brush could not be kept up and the cold made them shiver causing them to roam in the darkness along the desolate shore, back and forth, like restless ghouls. They seemed to fear their lives were in danger, and they must escape at any risk, and gradually worked themselves up to a determined struggle for life, though the only danger lay in seeking to leave the island. At length, after midnight, they could no longer be restrained and as the wind had slightly abated, I consented to try. We launched in safety and on we sped, keeping the boat squarely in the face of the wind to avoid upsetting. I, as pilot, sat in the bows to give warning of larger waves, one of my companions steered, and the other two rowed. . . . Seven miles to go. . . . The range to the south loomed dim and vast, and along the shore the Indians had built large encircling brush fire fences, for it was sage rabbit hunting time. These made a livid illumination, and dense black clouds of smoke were seen rising, making one think that after centuries of repose the volcanic cones were again bursting into action.

The wind howled, the waves broke repeatedly, and we had to bail to keep afloat. I sat with shoes unlaced, ready to swim, and feared not for life, as the water was not cold, though the dashing of bitter spray would be trying to the eyes. . . . Towards morning we got ashore and back to our camp in an old abandoned hut in the possession of wood rats. Yet it was a house, and all city visitors must have a roof over their heads. . . .

Thirst

June of 1878 found Muir in the wilderness of Nevada as part of a Coast and Geodetic Survey party headed by Captain A. F. Rodgers, who had led a similar expedition with Muir at Mount Shasta three years previously. Given Muir's many life-threatening adventures, to claim that in this instance he had "suffered as never before" is to suggest a miserable time, indeed. Muir's decision to undertake the climb of Lone Mountain, indeed any Nevada mountain, without sufficient water, is puzzling.

Muir, forty years of age, wrote this letter to the parents of Louie Wanda Strentzel, the woman with whom he was beginning a cautious courtship. They would marry two years later.

To Dr. and Mrs. John Strentzel

In camp near Belmont, Nevada
August 28th, 1878

I SENT YOU A NOTE FROM AUSTIN. Thence we traveled southward down the Big Smoky Valley, crossing and recrossing it between the Toyabe and Toquima Ranges, the dominating summits of which we ascended. Thence still southward towards Death Valley to Lone Mountain; thence northeastward to this little mining town.

From the summit of a huge volcanic table mountain of the Toquima Range I observed a truly glorious spectacle—a dozen "cloud-bursts" falling at once while we were cordially pelted with hail. The falling water cloud-drapery, thunder tones, lightning, and tranquil blue sky windows between made one of the most impressive pictures I ever beheld. One of these cloud-bursts fell upon Austin, another upon Eureka. But still more glorious to me was the big significant fact I found here, fresh, telling glacial phenomena—a whole series. Moraines, *roches moutonnées*, glacial sculptures, and even feeble specimens of glacier meadows and glacier lakes. I also observed less manifest glaciation on several other ranges. I have long guessed that this Great Basin was loaded with ice during the last cold period; but the rocks are as unresisting and the water spouts to which all the ranges have been exposed have not simply obscured the glacial scriptures here, but nearly buried and obliterated them, so that only the skilled observer would detect a single word, and he would probably be called a glaciated monomaniac. Now it is clear that this fiery inland region was icy prior to the lake period.

I have also been so fortunate as to settle that pine species we discussed, and found the nest and young of the Alpine sparrow. What do you think of all this—"A' that anda' that"? The sun heat has been intense. What a triangle of noses!—Captain Rodgers', Eimbeck's, and mine—mine sore, Eimbeck's sorer, Captain's sorest—scaled and dry as the backs of lizards, and divided into sections all over the surface and turned up on the edges like the surface layers of the desiccated sections of adobe flats.

On Lone Mountain we were *thirsty*. How we thought of the cool singing streams of the Sierra while our blood fevered and boiled and throbbed! Three of us ascended the mountain against my counsel and remonstrances while forty miles from any known water. Two of the three nearly lost their lives. I suffered least, though I suffered as never before, and was the only one strong enough to ascend a sandy cañon to find and fetch the animals after descending the mountain. Then I had to find my two companions. One I found death-like, lying in the hot sand, scarcely conscious and unable to speak above a frightful whisper. I managed, however, to get him on his horse. The other I found in a kind of delirious stupor, voiceless, in the sagebrush. It was a fearfully exciting search, and I forgot my own exhaustion in it, though I never for a moment lost my will and wits, or doubted our ability to endure and escape. We reached water at daybreak of the second day—two days and nights in this fire without water! A lesson has been learned that will last, and we will not suffer so again. Of course we could not eat or sleep all this time, for we could not swallow food and the fever prevented sleep. To-morrow we set out for the White Pine region.

Cordially yours
J. MUIR

The Rescue on Glenora Peak

Muir was the first to proclaim the significance of glacial activity on the Sierra Nevada landscape, and his vigorous explorations uncovered no less than sixty-five "small but living glaciers." In 1879 his enthusiasm for the subject was to take him to Alaska—the first of seven journeys to that territory. S. Hall Young, "fresh from college," was a Presbyterian minister assigned to the Thlinget Indians of Southeastern Alaska, and upon meeting Muir on a mail steamboat, established an instant and steadfast friendship.

WE REACHED THE OLD Hudson's Bay trading-post at Glenora about one o'clock, and the captain informed me that he would stop here until the next morning, when he would make an early start for Wrangell.

At a distance of about seven or eight miles to the northeastward of the landing, there is an outstanding group of mountains crowning a spur from the main chain of the Coast Range, whose highest point rises about eight thousand feet above the level of the sea; and as Glenora is only a thousand feet above the sea, the height to be overcome in climbing this peak is about seven thousand feet. Though the time was short I determined to climb it, because ot the advantageous position it occupied for general views of the peaks and glaciers of the east side of the great range.

Although it was now twenty minutes past three and the days were getting short, I thought that by rapid climbing I could reach the summit before sunset, in time to get general view and a few pencil sketches, and make my way back to the steamer in the night. Mr. Young, one of the missionaries, asked permission to accompany me, saying that he was a good walker and climber and would not delay me or cause any trouble. I strongly advised him not to go, explaining that it involved a walk, coming and going, of fourteen or sixteen miles, and a climb through brush and boulders of seven thousand feet, a fair day's work for a seasoned mountaineer to be done in less than half a day and part of a night. But he insisted that he was a strong walker, could do a mountaineer's day's work in half a day, and would not hinder me in any way.

"Well, I have warned you," I said, "and will not assume responsibility for any trouble that may arise."

He proved to be a stout walker, and we made rapid progress across a brushy timbered flat and up the mountain slopes, open in some places, and in others thatched with dwarf firs, resting a minute here and there to refresh ourselves with huckleberries, which grew in abundance in open spots. About half an hour before sunset, when we were near a cluster of crumbling pinnacles that formed the summit, I had ceased to feel anxiety about the mountaineering strength and skill of my companion, and pushed rapidly on. In passing around the shoulder of the highest pinnacle, where the rock was rapidly disintegrating and the danger of slipping was great, I shouted in a warning voice, "Be very careful here, this is dangerous."

Mr. Young was perhaps a dozen or two yards behind me, but out of sight. I afterwards reproached myself for not stopping and lending him a steadying hand, and showing the slight footsteps I had made by kicking out little blocks of the crumbling surface, instead of simply warning him to be careful. Only a few seconds after giving this warning, I was startled by a scream for help, and hurrying back, found the missionary face downward, his arms outstretched, clutching little crumbling knobs on the brink of a gully that plunges down a thousand feet or more to a small residual glacier. I managed to get below him, touched one of his feet, and tried to encourage him by saying, "I am below you. You are in no danger. You can't slip past me and I will soon get you out of this."

He then told me that both of his arms were dislocated. It was almost impossible to find available footholds on the treacherous rock, and I was at my wits' end to know how to get him rolled or dragged to a place where I could get about him, find out how much he was hurt, and a way back down the mountain. After narrowly scanning the cliff and making footholds, I managed to roll and lift him a few yards to a place where the slope was less steep, and there I attempted to set his arms. I found, however, that this was impossible in such a place. I therefore tied his arms to his sides with my suspenders and necktie, to prevent as much as possible inflammation from movement. I then left him, telling him to lie still, that I would be back in a few minutes, and that he was now safe from slipping. I hastily examined the ground and saw no way of getting him down except by the steep glacier gully. After scrambling to an outstanding point that commands a view of it from top to bottom, to make sure that it was not interrupted by sheer precipices, I concluded that with great care and the digging of slight footholds he could be slid down to the glacier, where I could lay him on his back and perhaps be able to set his arms. Accordingly, I cheered him up, telling him I had found a way, but that it would require lots of time and patience. Digging a footstep in the sand or crumbling rock five or six feet beneath him, I reached up, took hold of him by one of his feet, and gently slid him down on his back, placed his heels in the step, then descended another five or six feet, dug heel notches, and slid him down to them. Thus the whole distance was made by a succession of narrow steps at very short intervals, and the glacier was reached perhaps about midnight. Here I took off one of my boots, tied a handkerchief around his wrist for a good hold, placed my heel in his arm pit, and succeeded in getting one of his arms into place, but my utmost strength was insufficient to reduce the dislocation of the other. I therefore bound it closely to his side, and asked him if in his exhausted and trembling condition he was still able to walk.

"Yes," he bravely replied.

So, with a steadying arm around him and many stops for rest, I marched him slowly down in the starlight on the comparatively smooth, unfissured surface of the little glacier to the terminal moraine, a distance of perhaps a mile, crossed the moraine, bathed his head at one of the outlet streams, and after many rests reached a dry place and made a brush fire. I then went ahead looking for an open way through the bushes to where larger wood could be had, made a good lasting fire of resiny silver-fir roots, and a leafy bed beside it. I now told him I would run down the mountain, hasten back with help from the boat, and carry him down to comfort. But he would not hear of me leaving him.

"No, no," he said, "I can walk down. Don't leave me."

I reminded him of the roughness of the way, his nerve-shaken condition, and assured him I would not be gone long. But he insisted on trying, saying on no account whatever must I leave him. I therefore concluded to try to get him to the ship by short walks from one fire and resting-place to another. While he was resting I went ahead, looking for the best way through the brush and rocks, then returning, got him on his feet and made him lean on my shoulder while I steadied him to prevent his falling. This slow, staggering struggle from fire to fire lasted until long after sunrise. When at last we reached the ship and stood at the foot of the narrow single plank without side rails that reached from the bank to the deck at a considerable angle, I briefly explained to Mr. Young's companions, who stood looking down at us, that he had been hurt in an accident, and requested one of them to assist me in getting him aboard. But strange to say, instead of coming down to help, they made haste to reproach him for having gone on a "wild-goose chase" with Muir.

"These foolish adventures are well enough for Mr. Muir," they said, "but you, Mr. Young, have a work to do; you have a family; you have a church, and you have no right to risk your life on treacherous peaks and precipices."

The captain, Nat Lane, son of Senator Joseph Lane, had been swearing in angry impatience for being compelled to make so late a start and thus encounter a dangerous wind in a narrow gorge, and was threatening to put the missionaries ashore to seek their lost companion, while he went on down the river about his business. But when he heard my call for help, he hastened forward, and elbowed the divines away from the end of the gangplank, shouting in angry irreverence, "Oh, blank! This is no time for preaching! Don't you see this man is hurt?"

He ran down to our help, and while I steadied my trembling companion from behind, the captain kindly led him up the plank into the saloon, and made him drink a large glass of brandy. Then, with a man holding down his shoulders, we succeeded in getting the bone into its socket, notwithstanding the inflammation and contraction of the muscles and ligaments. Mr. Young was then put to bed, and he slept all the way back to Wrangell.

In his mission lectures in the East, Mr. Young oftentimes told this story. I made no record of it in my notebook and never intended to write a word about it; but after a miserable, sensational caricature of the story had appeared in a respectable magazine, I thought it fair to my brave companion that it should be told just as it happened.

Excerpted from *Travels in Alaska*. Boston and New York: Houghton Mifflin Company, 1915.

REVEREND YOUNG'S VERSION

Though there are many independent observations of Muir's character and of his mountaineering skills, none give us a more detailed look than S. Hall Young's Alaska Days with John Muir, *published in 1915.*

Dropping down from Telegraph Creek (so named because it was a principal station of the great projected trans-American and trans-Siberian line of the Western Union, that bubble pricked by Cyrus Field's cable), we tied up at Glenora about noon of a cloudless day.

"Amuse yourselves," said Captain Lane at lunch. "Here we stay till two o'clock tomorrow morning. This gale, blowing from the sea, makes safe steering through the Canyon impossible, unless we take the morning's calm."

I saw Muir's eyes light up with a peculiar meaning as he glanced quickly at me across the table. He knew the leading strings I was in; how those well-meaning D.D.s and their motherly wives thought they had a special mission to suppress all my self-destructive proclivities toward dangerous adventure, and especially to protect me from "that wild Muir" and his hare-brained schemes of mountain climbing.

"Where is it?" I asked, as we met behind the pilot house a moment later.

He pointed to a little group of jagged peaks rising right up from where we stood—a pulpit in the center of a vast rotunda of magnificent mountains. "One of the finest viewpoints in the world," he said.

"How far to the highest point?"

"About ten miles."

"How high?"

"Seven or eight thousand feet."

That was enough. I caught the D.D.s with guile. There were Stickeen Indians there catching salmon, and among them Chief Shakes, who our interpreter said was "The youngest but the headest Chief of all." Last night's palaver had whetted the appetites of both sides for more. On the part of the Indians, a talk with "Great White Chiefs from Washington" offered unlimited possiblities for material favor; and to the good divines the "simple faith and childlike docility" of these children of the forest were a constant delight. And then how well their high-flown compliments and flowery metaphors would sound in article and speech to the wondering East! So I sent Stickeen Johnny, the interpreter, to call the natives to another *hyou wawa* (big talk) and, note-book in hand, the doctors "went gayly to the fray." I set the speeches a-going, and then slipped out to join the impatient Muir.

"Take off your coat," he commanded, "and here's your supper."

Pocketing two hardtacks apiece we were off, keeping in shelter of house and bush till out of sight of the council-house and the flower-picking ladies. Then we broke out. What a matchless climate! What sweet, lung-filling air! Sunshine that had no weakness in it—as if we were springing plants. Our sinews like steel springs, muscles like India rubber, feet soled with iron to grip the rocks. Ten miles? Eight thousand feet? Why, I felt equal to forty miles and the Matterhorn!

"Eh, mon!" said Muir, lapsing into the broad Scotch he was so fond of using when enjoying himself, "ye'll see the sicht o' yer life the day. Ye'll get that'll be o' mair use till ye than a' the gowd o' Cassiar."

From the first, it was a hard climb. Fallen timber at the mountain's foot covered with thick brush swallowed us up and plucked us back. Beyond, on the steeper slopes, grew dwarf evergreens, five or six feet high—the same fir that towers a hundred feet with a diameter of three of four on the river banks, but here stunted by icy mountain winds. The curious blasting of the branches on the side next to the mountain gave them the appearance of long-armed, hump-backed, hairy gnomes, bristling with anger, stretching forbidding arms downwards to bar our passage to their sacred heights. Sometimes an inviting vista through the branches would lure us in, when it would narrow, and at its upper angle we would find a solid phalanx of these grumpy dwarfs. Then we had to attack boldly, scrambling over the obstinate, elastic arms and against the clusters of stiff needles, till we gained the upper side and found another green slope.

Muir led, of course, picking with sure instinct the easiest way. Three hours of steady work brought us suddenly beyond the timber-line, and the real joy of the day began. Nowhere else have I seen anything approaching the luxuriance and variety of delicate blossoms shown by these high, mountain pastures of the North. "You scarce could see the grass for flowers." Everything that was marvelous in form, fair in color, or sweet in fragrance seemed to be represented there, from daisies and campanulas to Muir's favorite, the cassiope, with its exquisite little pink-white bells shaped like lilies-of-the-valley and its subtle perfume. Muir at once went wild when we reached this fairyland. From cluster to cluster of flowers he ran, falling on his knees, babbling in unknown tongues, prattling a curious mixture of scientific lingo and baby talk, worshiping his little blue-

and-pink goddesses.

"Ah! my blue-eyed darlin', little did I think to see you here. How did you stray away from Shasta?"

"Well, well! Who'd 'a' thought that you'd have left that niche in the Merced mountains to come here!"

"And who might you be, now, with your wonder look? Is it possible that you can be (two Latin polysyllables)? You're lost, my dear; you belong in Tennessee."

"Ah! I thought I'd find you, my homely little sweetheart," and so on unceasingly.

So absorbed was he in this amatory botany that he seemed to forget my existence. While I, as glad as he, tagged along, running up and down with him, asking now and then a question, learning something of plant life, but far more of that spiritual insight into Nature's lore which is granted only to those who love and woo her in her great outdoor palaces. But how I anathematized my short-sighted foolishness for having as a student at old Wooster shirked botany for the "more important" studies of language and metaphysics. For here was a man whose natural science had a thorough technical basis, while the super-structure was built of "lively stones," and was itself a living temple of love!

With all his boyish enthusiasm, Muir was a most painstaking student; and any unsolved question lay upon his mind like a personal grievance until it was settled to his full understanding. One plant after another, with its sand-covered roots, went into his pockets, his handkerchief and the "full" of his shirt until he was bulbing and sprouting all over, and could carry no more. He was taking them to the boat to analyze and compare at leisure. Then he began to requisition my receptacles. I stood it while he stuffed my pockets, but rebelled when he tried to poke the prickly, scratchy things inside my shirt. I had not yet attained that sublime indifference to physical comfort, that Nirvana of passivity, that Muir had found.

Hours had passed in this entrancing work and we were progressing upwards but slowly. We were on the southeastern slope of the mountain, and the sun was still staring at us from a cloudless sky. Suddenly we were in shadow as we worked around a spur of rock. Muir looked up, startled. Then he jammed home his last handful of plants, and hastened up to where I stood.

"Man!" he said, "I was forgetting. We'll have to hurry now or we'll miss it, we'll miss it."

"Miss what?" I asked.

"The jewel of the day," he answered; "the sight of the sunset from the top."

Then Muir began to *slide* up that mountain. I had been with mountain climbers before, but never one like him. A deer-lope over the smoother slopes, a sure instinct for the easiest way into a rocky fortress, an instant and unerring attack, a serpent-glide up the steep; eye, hand and foot all connected dynamically; with no appearance of weight to his body—as though he had Stockton's negative gravity machine strapped on his back.

Fifteen years of enthusiastic study among the Sierras had given him the same preeminance over the ordinary climber as the Big Horn of the Rockies shows over the Cotswold. It was only for exerting myself to the limits of my strength that I was able to keep near him. His example was at the same time my inspiration and despair. I longed for him to stop and rest, but would not have suggested it for the world. I would at least be game, and furnish no hint as to how tired I was, no matter how chokingly my heart thumped. Muir's spirit was in me, and my "chief end," just then, was to win that peak with him. The impending calamity of being beaten by the sun was not to be contemplated without horror. The loss of a fortune would be as nothing to that!

We were now beyond the flower garden of the gods, in a land of rocks and cliffs, with patches of short grass, caribou moss and lichens between. Along a narrowing arm of the mountain, a deep canyon flumed a rushing torrent of icy water from a small glacier on our right. Then came moraine matter, rounded pebbles and boulders, and beyond them the glacier. Once a giant, it is nothing but a baby now, but the ice is still blue and clear, and the crevasses many and deep. And that day it had to be crossed, which was a ticklish task. A misstep or slip might land us at once fairly into the heart of the glacier, there to be preserved in cold storage for the wonderment of future generations. But glaciers were Muir's special pets, his intimate companions, with whom he held sweet communion. Their voices were plain language to his ears, their work, as God's landscape gardeners, of the wisest and best that Nature could offer.

No Swiss guide was ever wiser in the habits of glaciers than Muir, or proved to be a better pilot across their deathly crevasses. Half a mile of careful walking and jumping and we were on the ground again, at the base of the great cliff of metamorphic slate that crowned the summit. Muir's aneroid barometer showed a height of about seven thousand feet, and the wall of rock towered threateningly above us, leaning out in places, a thousand feet or so above the glacier. But the earth-fires that had melted and heaved it, the ice mass that chiseled and shaped it, the wind and rain that corroded and crumbled it, had left plenty of bricks out of that battlement, had covered its face with knobs and horns, had ploughed ledges and cleaved fissures and fastened crags and pinnacles upon it, so that, while its surface was full of man-traps and blind ways, the human spider might still find some hold for his claws.

The shadows were dark upon us, but the lofty, icy peaks of the main range still lay bathed in the golden rays of the setting sun. There was no time to be lost. A quick glance to the right and left, and Muir, who had steered his course wisely across the glacier, attacked the cliff, simply saying, "We must climb cautiously here."

Now came the most wonderful display of his mountain-craft. Had I been alone at the feet of these crags I should have said, "It can't be done," and have turned back down the mountain. But Muir was my "control," as the Spiritists say, and I never thought of doing anything else but following him. He thought he could climb up there and that settled it. He would do what he thought he could. And such climbing! There was never an instant when both feet and hands were not in play, and often elbows, knees, thighs, upper arms, and even chin must grip and hold. Clambering up a steep slope, crawling under an overhanging rock, spreading out like a flying squirrel and edging along an inch-wide projection while fingers clasped knobs above the head, bending about sharp angles, pulling up smooth rock-faces by sheer strength of arm and chinning over the edge, leaping fissures, sliding flat around a dangerous rock-breast, testing crumbly spurs before risking his weight, always going up, up, no hesitation, no pause—that was Muir! My task was the lighter one; he did the head-work, I had but to imitate. The thin fragment of projecting slate that stood the weight of his one hundred and fifty pounds would surely sustain my hundred and thirty. As far as possible I did as he did, took his handholds, and stepped in his steps.

But I was handicapped in a way that Muir was ignorant of, and I would not tell him for fear of his veto upon my climbing. My legs were all right—hard and sinewy; my body light and supple, my wind good, my nerves steady (heights did not make me dizzy); but my arms—there lay the trouble. Ten years before I had been fond of breaking colts—till the colts broke me. On successive summers in West Virginia, two colts had fallen with me and dislocated first my left shoulder, then my right. Since then both arms had been out of joint more than once. My left was especially weak. It would not sustain my weight, and I had to favor it constantly. Now and again, as I pulled myself up some difficult reach I could feel the head of the humerous move from its socket.

Muir climbed so fast that his movements were almost like flying, legs and arms moving with perfect precision and unfailing judgment. I must keep close behind him or I would fail to see his points of vantage. But the pace was a killing one for me. As we neared the summit my strength began to fail, my breath to come in gasps, my muscles to twitch. The overwhelming fear of losing sight of my guide, of being left behind and failing to see that sunset, grew upon me, and I hurled myself blindly at every fresh obstacle, determined to keep up. At length we climbed upon a little shelf, a foot or two wide, that corkscrewed to the left. Here we paused a moment to take breath and look around us. We had ascended the cliff some nine hundred and fifty feet from the glacier, and were within forty or fifty feet of the top.

Among the much-prized gifts of this good world one of the very richest was given to me in that hour. It is securely locked in the safe of my memory and nobody can rob me of it—an imperishable treasure. Standing out on the rounded neck of the cliff and facing the southwest, we could see on three sides of us. The view was much the finest of all my experience. We seemed to stand on a high rostrum in the center of the greatest amphitheater in the world. The sky was cloudless, the level sun flooding all the landscape with golden light. From the base of the mountain on which we stood stretched the rolling upland. Striking boldly across our front was the deep valley of the Stickeen, a line of foliage, light green cottonwoods and darker alders, sprinkled with black fir and spruce, through which the river gleamed with a silvery sheen, now spreading wide among its islands, now foaming white through narrow canyons. Beyond, among the undulating hills, was a marvelous array of lakes. There must have been thirty or forty of them, from the pond of an acre to the wide sheet two or three miles across. The strangely elongated and rounded hills had the appearance of giants in bed, wrapped in many-colored blankets, while the lakes were their deep, blue eyes, lashed with dark evergreens, gazing steadfastly heavenward. Look long at these recumbent forms and you will see the heaving of their breasts.

The whole landscape was alert, expectant of glory. Around this great camp of prostrate Cyclops there stood an unbroken semicircle of mighty peaks in solemn grandeur, some hoary-headed, some with locks of brown, but all wearing white glacier collars. The taller peaks seemed almost sharp enough to be the helmets and spears of watchful sentinels. And the colors! Great stretches of crimson fireweed, acres and acres of them, smaller patches of dark blue lupins, and hills of shaded yellow, red, and brown, the many-shaded green of the woods, the amethyst and purple of the far horizon—who can tell it? We did not stand there more than two or three minutes, but the whole wonderful scene is deeply etched on the tablet of my memory, a photogravure never to be effaced.

Muir was the first to awake from his trance. Like Schiller's king in "The Diver," "Nothing could slake his wild thirst of desire."

"The sunset," he cried; "we must have the whole horizon."

Then he started running along the ledge like a mountain goat, working to get around the vertical cliff above us to find an ascent on the other side. He was soon out of sight, although I followed as fast as I could. I heard him shout something, but could not make out his words. I know now he was warning me of a dangerous place. Then I came to a sharp-cut fissure which lay across my path—a gash in the rock, as if one of the Cyclops had struck it with his axe. It sloped very steeply for some twelve feet below, opening on the face of the precipice above the glacier, and was filled to within about four feet of the surface with flat, slaty gravel. It was only four or five feet across, and I could easily have leaped it had I not been so tired. But a rock the size of my head projected from the slippery stream of gravel. In my haste to overtake Muir I did not stop to make sure this stone was part of the cliff, but stepped with springing force upon it to cross the fissure. Instantly the stone melted away beneath my feet, and I shot with it down towards the precipice. With my peril sharp upon me I cried out as I whirled on my face, and struck out both hands to grasp the rock on either side.

Falling forward hard, my hands struck the walls of the chasm, my arms were twisted behind me, and instantly both shoulders were dislocated. With my paralyzed arms flopping helplessly above my head, I slid swiftly down the narrow chasm. Instinctively I flattened down on the sliding gravel, digging my chin and toes into it to check my descent; but not until my feet hung out over the edge of the cliff did I feel that I had stopped. Even then I dared not breathe or stir, so precarious was my hold on that treacherous shale. Every moment I seemed to be slipping inch by inch to the point when all would give way and I would go whirling down to the glacier.

After the first wild moment of panic when I felt myself falling, I do not remember any sense of fear. But I know what it is to have a thousand thoughts flash through the brain in a single instant—an anguished thought of my young wife at Wrangell, with her imminent motherhood; an indignant thought of the insurance companies that refused me policies on my life; a thought of wonder as to what would become of my poor flocks of Indians among the islands; recollections of events far and near in time, important and trivial; but each thought printed upon my memory by the instantaneous photography of deadly peril. I had no hope of escape at all. The gravel was rattling past me and piling up against my head. The jar of a little rock, and all would be over. The situation was too desperate for actual fear. Dull wonder as to how long I would be in the air, and the hope that death would be instant—that was all. Then came the wish that Muir would come before I fell, and take a message to my wife.

Suddenly, I heard his voice right above me. "My God!" he cried. Then he added, "Grab that rock, man just by your right hand."

I gurgled from my throat, not daring to inflate my lungs, "My arms are out."

There was a pause. Then his voice rang again, cheery, confident, unexcited, "Hold fast; I'm going to get you out of this. I can't get to you on this side; the rock is sheer. I'll have to leave you now and cross the rift high up and come down to you on the other side by which we came. Keep cool."

Then I heard him going away, whistling "The Blue Bells of Scotland," singing snatches of Scotch songs, calling to me, his voice now receding, as the rocks intervened, then sounding louder as he came out on the face of the cliff. But in me hope surged at full tide. I entertained no more thoughts of last messages. I did not see how he could possibly do it, but he was John Muir, and I had seen his wonderful rock-work. So I determined not to fall and made myself as flat and heavy as possible, not daring to twitch a muscle or wink an eyelid, for I still felt myself slipping, slipping down the greasy slate. And now a new peril threatened. A chill ran through me of cold and nervousness, and I slid an inch. I suppressed the growing shivers with all my will. I would keep perfectly still till Muir came back. The sickening pain in my shoulders increased till it was torture, and I could not ease it.

It seemed like hours, but it was really only about ten minutes before he got back to me. By that time I hung so far over the edge of the precipice that it seemed impossible that I could last another second. Now, I heard

Muir's voice, low and steady, close to me, and it seemed a little below.

"Hold steady," he said. "I'll have to swing you out over the cliff."

Then I felt a careful hand on my back, fumbling with the waistband of my pants, my vest and shirt, gathering all in a firm grip. I could see only with one eye and that looked upon but a foot or two of gravel on the other side.

"Now!" he said, and I slid out of the cleft with a rattling shower of stones and gravel. My head swung down, my impotent arms dangling, and I stared straight at the glacier, a thousand feet below. Then my feet came against the cliff.

"Work downwards with your feet."

I obeyed. He drew me close to him by crooking his arm and as my head came up past his level he caught me by my collar with his teeth! My feet struck the little two-inch shelf on which he was standing, and I could see Muir, flattened against the face of the rock and facing it, his right hand stretched up and clasping a little spur, his left holding me with an iron grip, his head bent sideways, as my weight drew it. I felt as alert and cool as he.

"I've got to let go of you," he hissed through his clenched teeth. "I need both hands here. Climb upward with your feet."

How he did it, I know not. The miracle grows as I ponder it. The wall was almost perpendicular and smooth. My weight on his jaws dragged him outwards. And yet, holding me by his teeth as a panther her cub and clinging like a squirrel to a tree, he climbed with me straight up ten or twelve feet, with only help of my iron-shod feet scrambling on the rock. It was utterly impossible, yet he did it!

When he landed me on the little shelf along which we had come, my nerve gave way and I trembled all over. I sank down exhausted, Muir only less tired, but supporting me.

The sun had set; the air was icy cold and we had no coats. We would soon chill through. Muir's task of rescue had only begun and no time was to be lost. In a minute he was up again, examining my shoulders. The right one had an upward dislocation, the ball of the humerus resting on the process of the scapula, the rim of the cup. I told him how, and he soon snapped the bone into its socket. But the left was a harder proposition. The luxation was downward and forward, and the strong, nervous reaction of the muscles had pulled the head of the bone deep into my armpit. There was no room to work on that narrow ledge. All that could be done was to make a rude sling with one of my suspenders and our handkerchiefs, so as to both support the elbow and keep the arm from swinging.

Then came the task to get down that terrible wall to the glacier, by the only practicable way down the mountain that Muir, after a careful search, could find. Again I am at a loss to know how he accomplished it. For an unencumbered man to descend it in the deepening dusk was a most difficult task; but to get a tottery, nerve-shaken, pain-wracked cripple down was a feat of positive wonder. My right arm, though in place, was almost helpless. I could only move my forearm; the muscles of the upper part simply refusing to obey my will. Muir would let himself down to a lower shelf, brace himself, and I would get my right hand against him, crawl my fingers over his shoulder until the arm hung in front of him, and falling against him, would be eased down to his standing ground. Sometimes he would pack me a short distance on his back. Again, taking me by the wrist, he would swing me down to a lower shelf, before descending himself. My right shoulder came out three times that night, and had to be reset.

It was dark when we reached the base; there was no moon and it was very cold. The glacier provided an operating table, and I lay on the ice for an hour while Muir, having slit the sleeve of my shirt to the collar, tugged and twisted at my left arm in a vain attempt to set it. But the ball was too deep in its false socket, and all his pulling only bruised and made it swell. So he had to do up the arm again, and tie it tight to my body. It must have been near midnight when we left the foot of the cliff and started down the mountain. We had ten hard miles to go, and no supper, for the hardtack had disappeared ere we were half-way up the mountain. Muir dared not take me across the glacier in the dark; I was too weak to jump the crevasses. So we skirted it and came, after a mile, to the head of a great slide of gravel; I sat against him with my feet on either side and my arm over his shoulder. Then he began to hitch and kick, and presently we were sliding at great speed in a cloud of dust. A full half-mile we flew, and were almost buried when we reached the bottom of the slide. It was the easiest part of our trip.

Now we found ourselves in the canyon, down which tumbled the glacial stream, and far beneath the ridge along which we had ascended. The sides of the canyon were sheer cliffs.

"We'll try it," said Muir. "Sometimes these canyons are passable."

But the way grew rougher as we descended. The rapids became falls and we often had to retrace our steps to find a way around them. After we reached the timber-line, some four miles from the summit, the going was still harder, for we had a thicket of alders and willows to fight. Here Muir offered to make a fire and leave me while he went forward for assistance, but I refused. "No," I said, "I'm going to make it to the boat."

All that night this man of steel and lightning worked, never resting a minute, doing the work of three men, helping me along the slopes, easing me down the rocks, pulling me up cliffs, dashing water on me when I grew faint with the pain; and always cheery, full of talk and anecdote, cracking jokes with me, infusing me with his own indomitable spirit. He was eyes, hands, feet, and heart to me—my caretaker, in whom I trusted absolutely. My eyes brim with tears even now when I think of his utter self-abandon as he ministered to my infirmities.

About four o'clock in the morning, we came to a fall that we could not compass, sheer a hundred feet or more. So we had to attack the steep walls of the canyon. After a hard struggle we were on the mountain ridges again, traversing the flower pastures, creeping through openings in the brush, scrambling over the dwarf fir, then down through the fallen timber. It was half-past seven o'clock when we descended the last slope and found the path to Glenora. Here we met a straggling party of whites and Indians just starting out to search the mountains for us.

As I was coming wearily up the teetering gang-plank, feeling as if I couldn't keep up another minute, Dr. Kendall stepped upon its end, barring my passage, bent his bushy white brows upon me from his six feet of height, and began to scold:

"See here, young man; give an account of yourself. Do you know you've kept us waiting—"

Just then Captain Lane jumped forward to help me, digging the old

Doctor of Divinity with his elbow in the stomach and nearly knocking him off the boat.

"Oh, hell!" he roared. "Can't you see the man's hurt?"

Mrs. Kendall was a very tall, thin, severe-looking old lady, with face lined with grief by the loss of her children. She never smiled. She had not gone to bed at all that night, but walked the deck and would not let her husband or the others sleep. Soon after daylight she began to lash the men with the whip of her tongue for their "cowardice and inhumanity" in not starting at once to search for me.

"Mr. Young is undoubtedly lying mangled at the foot of a cliff, or else one of those terrible bears has wounded him; and you are lolling around here instead of starting to his rescue. For shame!"

When they objected that they did not know where we had gone, she snapped: "Go everywhere until you find him."

Her fierce energy started the men we met. When I came on board she at once took charge and issued her orders, which everybody jumped to obey. She had blankets spread on the floor of the cabin and laid me on them. She obtained some whisky from the captain, some water, porridge and coffee from the steward. She was sitting on the floor with my head in her lap, feeding me coffee with a spoon, when Dr. Kendall came in and began on me again:

"Suppose you had fallen down that precipice, what would your poor wife have done? What would have become of your Indians and your new church?"

Then Mrs. Kendall turned and thrust her spoon like a sword at him. "Henry Kendall," she blazed, "shut right up and leave this room. Have you no sense? Go instantly, I say!" And the good Doctor went.

My recollections of that day are not very clear. The shoulder was in a bad condition—swollen, bruised, very painful. I had to be strengthened with food and rest, and Muir called from his sleep of exhaustion, so that with four other men he could pull and twist that poor arm of mine for an hour. They got it into its socket, but scarcely had Muir got to sleep again before the strong, nervous twitching of the shoulder dislocated it a second time and seemingly placed it in a worse condition than before. Captain Lane was now summoned, and with Muir to direct, they worked for two or three hours. Whisky was poured down my throat to relax my stubborn, pain-convulsed muscles. Then they went at it with two men pulling at the towel knotted about my wrist, two others pulling against them, foot braced to foot, Muir manipulating my shoulder with his sinewy hands, and the stocky Captain, strong and compact as a bear, with his heel against the yarn ball in my armpit, takes me by the elbow and says, "I'll set it or pull the arm off!"

Well, he almost does the latter. I am conscious of a frightful strain, a spasm of anguish in my side as his heel slips from the ball and kicks in two of my ribs, a snap as the head of the bone slips into the cup—then kindly oblivion.

I was awakened about five o'clock in the afternoon by the return of the whole party from an excursion to the Great Glacier at the Boundary Line. Muir, fresh and enthusiastic as ever, had been the pilot across the moraine and upon the great ice mountain; and I, wrapped like a mummy in linen strips, was able to join in his laughter as he told of the big D.D.'s heroics, when, in the middle of an acre of alder brush, he asked indignantly, in response to the hurry-up calls: "Do you think I'm going to leave my wife in this forest?"

One overpowering regret—one only—abides in my heart as I think back upon that golden day with John Muir. He could, and did, go back to Glenora on the return trip of the *Cassiar*, ascend the mountain again, see the sunset from its top, make charming sketches, stay all night and see the sunrise, filling his cup of joy so full that he could pour out entrancing descriptions for days. While I—well, with entreating arms about one's neck and pleading, tearful eyes looking into one's own, what could one do but promise to climb no more? But my lifeling lamentation over a treasure forever lost, is this: "I never saw the sunset from that peak."

Excerpted from *Alaska Days with John Muir* by S. Hall Young. New York, Chicago, Toronto: Fleming H. Revell Company, 1915.

Stickeen

The icy storm story of a little dog named Stickeen, owned by S. Hall Young, was and is still perhaps the most popular and most loved of Muir's many adventures. This version of the story, which offers a bit less of the dog and more of the adventure, is taken from Travels in Alaska. *A longer and more complete rendition called "An Adventure with a Dog and a Glacier" was first published by* Century Magazine *in 1897. Muir rewrote this classic story many times, until it finally appeared in book form in 1909.*

The "funny, black, short-legged, bunchy-bodied, toy-dog," as he described Stickeen, gave Muir valuable insights into our kinship with all of our "earth-born companions." In his journals Muir wrote, "Anyhow, we were nearly killed and we both learned a lesson never to be forgotten, and are better man and dog for it—learned that human love and animal love, hope and fear, are essentially the same, derived from the same sources, and fall on all alike like sunshine." The adventure took place during Muir's second trip to Alaska in 1880, on the Taylor Glacier, west of Glacier Bay.

I SET OFF EARLY THE MORNING OF August 30 before anyone else in camp had stirred, not waiting for breakfast, but only eating a piece of bread. I had intended getting a cup of coffee, but a wild storm was blowing and calling, and I could not wait. Running out against the rain-laden gale and turning to catch my breath, I saw that the minister's little dog had left his bed in the tent and was coming boring through the storm, evidently determined to follow me. I told him to go back, that such a day as this had nothing for him.

"Go back," I shouted, "and get your breakfast." But he simply stood with his head down, and when I began to urge my way again, looking around, I saw he was still following me. So I at last told him to come on if he must and gave him a piece of bread I had in my pocket.

Instead of falling, the rain, mixed with misty shreds of clouds, was flying in level sheets, and the wind was roaring as I had never heard the wind roar before. Over the icy levels and over the woods, on the mountains, over the jagged rocks and spires and chasms of the glacier it boomed and moaned and roared, filling the fiord in even, gray, structureless gloom, inspiring and awful. I first struggled up in the face of the blast to the east end of the ice-wall, where a patch of forest had been carried away by the glacier when it was advancing. I noticed a few stumps well out on the moraine flat, showing that its present bare, raw condition was not the condition of fifty or a hundred years ago. In front of this part of the glacier there is a small moraine lake about half a mile in length, around the margin of which are a considerable number of trees standing knee-deep, and of course dead. This also is a result of the recent advance of the ice.

Pushing up through the ragged edge of the woods on the left margin of the glacier, the storm seemed to increase in violence, so that it was difficult to draw breath in facing it; therefore I took shelter back of a tree to enjoy it and wait, hoping that it would at last somewhat abate. Here the glacier, descending over an abrupt rock, falls forward in grand cascades, while a stream swollen by the rain was now a torrent,—wind, rain, ice-torrent, and water-torrent in one grand symphony.

At length the storm seemed to abate somewhat, and I took off my heavy rubber boots, with which I had waded the glacial streams on the flat, and laid them with my overcoat on a log, where I might find them on my way back, knowing I would be drenched anyhow, and firmly tied my mountain shoes, tightened my belt, shouldered my ice-axe, and, thus free and ready for rough work, pushed on, regardless as possible of mere rain. Making my way up a steep granite slope, its projecting polished bosses encumbered here and there by boulders and the ground and bruised ruins of the ragged edge of the forest that had been uprooted by the glacier during its recent advance, I traced the side of the glacier for two or three miles, finding everywhere evidence of its having encroached on the woods, which here run back along its edge for fifteen or twenty miles. Under the projecting edge of this vast ice-river I could see down beneath it to a depth of fifty feet or so in some places, where logs and branches were being crushed to pulp, some of it almost fine enough for paper, though most of it stringy and coarse.

After thus tracing the margin of the glacier for three or four miles, I chopped steps and climbed to the top, and as far as the eye could reach, the nearly level glacier stretched indefinitely away in the gray cloudy sky, a prairie of ice. The wind was now almost moderate, though rain continued to fall, which I did not mind, but a tendency to mist in the drooping draggled clouds made me hesitate about attempting to cross to the opposite shore. Although the distance was only six or seven miles, no traces at this time could be seen of the mountains on the other side, and in case the sky should grow darker, as it seemed inclined to do, I feared that when I got out of sight of land and perhaps into a maze of crevasses I might find difficulty in winning a way back.

Lingering a while and sauntering about in sight of the shore, I found this eastern side of the glacier remarkably free from large crevasses. Nearly all I met were so narrow I could step across them almost anywhere, while the few wide ones were easily avoided by going up or down along their sides to where they narrowed. The dismal cloud ceiling showed rifts here and there, and, thus encouraged, I struck out for the west shore, aiming to strike it five or six miles above the front wall, cautiously taking compass bearings at short intervals to enable me to find my way back should the weather darken again with mist or rain or snow. The structure lines of the glacier itself were, however, my main guide. All went well. I came to a deeply furrowed section about two miles in width where I had to zigzag in long, tedious tacks and make narrow doublings, tracing the edges of wide longitudinal furrows and chasms until I could find a bridge connecting their sides, oftentimes making the direct distance ten times over. The walking was good of its kind, however, and by dint of patient doubling and axe-work on dangerous places, I gained the opposite shore in about three hours, the width of the glacier at this point being about seven miles. Occasionally, while making my way, the clouds lifted a little, revealing a few bald, rough mountains sunk to the throat in the broad, icy sea which encompassed them on all sides, sweeping on forever and forever as we count time, wearing them away, giving them the shape they are destined to take when in the fullness of time they shall be parts of new landscapes.

Ere I lost sight of the east-side mountains, those on the west came into sight, so that holding my course was easy, and, though making haste, I halted for a moment to gaze down into the beautiful pure blue crevasses and to drink at the lovely blue wells, the most beautiful of all Nature's water-basins, or at the rills and streams outspread over the ice-land prairie, never ceasing to admire their lovely color and music as they glided and swirled in their blue crystal channels and potholes, and the rumbling of the moulins, or mills, where streams poured into blue-walled pits of unknown depth, some of them as regularly circular as if bored with augers. Interesting, too, were the cascades over blue cliffs, where streams fell into crevasses or slid almost noiselessly down slopes so smooth and frictionless their motion was concealed. The round or oval wells, however, from one to ten feet wide, and from one to twenty or thirty feet deep, were perhaps the most beautiful of all, the water so pure as to be almost invisible. My widest views did not probably exceed fifteen miles, the rain and mist making distances seem greater.

On reaching the farther shore and tracing it a few miles to northward, I found a large portion of the glacier-current sweeping out westward in a bold and beautiful curve around the shoulder of a mountain as if going direct to the open sea. Leaving the main trunk, it breaks into a magnificent uproar of pinnacles and spires and up-heaving, splashing wave-shaped masses, a crystal cataract incomparable, greater and wilder than a score of Niagaras.

Tracing its channel three or four miles, I found that it fell into a lake, which it fills with bergs. The front of this branch of the glacier is about three miles wide. I first took the lake to be the head of an arm of the sea, but going down to its shore and tasting it, I found it fresh, and by my aneroid perhaps less than a hundred feet above sea level. It is probably separated from the sea only by a moraine dam. I had not time to go around its shores, as it was now near five o'clock and I was about fifteen miles from camp, and I had to make haste to recross the glacier before dark, which would come on about eight o'clock. I therefore made haste up to the main glacier, and, shaping my course by compass and the structure lines of the ice, set off from the land out on to the grand crystal prairie again. All was so silent and so concentrated, owing to the low dragging mist, the beauty close about me was all the more keenly felt, though tinged with a dim sense of danger, as if coming events were casting shadows. I was soon out of sight of land, and the evening dusk that on cloudy days precedes the real night gloom came stealing on and only ice was in sight, and the only sounds, save the low rumbling of the mills and the rattle of falling stones at long intervals, were the low, terribly earnest moanings of the wind or distant waterfalls coming through the thickening gloom. After two hours of hard work I came to a maze of crevasses of appalling depth and width which could not be passed apparently either up or down. I traced them with firm nerve developed by the danger, making wide jumps, poising cautiously on dizzy edges after cutting footholds, taking wide crevasses at a grand leap at once frightful and inspiring. Many a mile was thus traveled, mostly up and down the glacier, making but little real headway, running much of the time as the danger of having to pass the night on the ice became more and more imminent. This I could do, though with the weather and my rain-soaked condition it would be trying at best. In treading the mazes of this crevassed section I had frequently to cross bridges that were only knife-edges for twenty or thirty feet, cutting off the sharp tops and leaving them flat so that little Stickeen could follow me. These I had to straddle, cutting off the top as I progressed and hitching gradually ahead like a boy riding a rail fence. All this time the little dog followed me bravely, never hesitating on the brink of any crevasse that I had jumped, but now that it was becoming dark and the crevasses became more troublesome, he followed close at my heels instead of scampering far and wide, where the ice was at all smooth, as he had in the forenoon. No land was now in sight. The mist fell lower and darker and snow began to fly. I could not see far enough up and down the glacier to judge how best to work out of the bewildering labyrinth, and how hard I tried while there was yet hope of reaching camp that night! a hope which was fast growing dim like the sky. After dark, on such ground, to keep from freezing, I could only jump up and down until morning on a piece of flat ice between the crevasses, dance to the boding music of the winds and waters, and as I was already tired and hungry I would be in bad condition for such ice work. Many times I was put to my mettle, but with a firm-braced nerve, all the more unflinching as the dangers thickened, I worked out of that terrible ice-web, and with blood fairly up Stickeen and I ran over common danger without fatigue. Our very hardest trial was in getting across the very last of the sliver bridges. After examining the first of the two widest crevasses, I followed its edge half a mile or so up and down and discovered that its narrowest spot was about eight feet wide, which was the limit of what I was able to jump. Moreover, the side I was on—that is, the west side—was about a foot higher than the other, and I feared that in case I should be stopped by a still wider impassable crevasse ahead that I would hardly be able to take back that jump from its lower side. The ice beyond, however, as far as I could see it, looked temptingly smooth. Therefore, after carefully making a socket for my foot on the rounded brink, I jumped, but found that I had nothing to spare and more than ever dreaded having to retrace my way. Little Stickeen jumped this, however, without apparently taking a second look at it, and we ran ahead joyfully over smooth, level ice, hoping we were now leaving all danger behind us. But hardly had we gone a hundred or two yards when to our dismay we found ourselves on the very widest of all the longitudinal crevasses we had yet encountered. It was about forty feet wide. I ran anxiously up the side of it to northward, eagerly hoping that I could get around its head, but my worst fears were realized when at a distance of about a mile or less it ran into the crevasse I had just jumped. I then ran down the edge for a mile or more below the point where I had first met it, and found that its lower end also united with the crevasse I had jumped, showing dismally that we were on an island two or three hundred yards wide and about two miles long and the only way of escape from this island was by turning back and jumping again that crevasse which I dreaded, or venturing ahead across the giant crevasse by the very worst of the sliver bridges I had ever seen. It was so badly weathered and melted down that it formed a knife-edge, and extended across from side to side in a low, drooping curve like that made by a loose rope attached at each end at the same height. But the worst difficulty was that the ends of the down-curving sliver were attached to the sides at a depth of about eight or ten feet below the surface of the glacier. Getting down to the end of the bridge, and then after crossing it getting up the other side, seemed hardly possible. However, I decided to dare the dangers of the fearful sliver rather than to attempt to retrace my steps. Accordingly I dug a low groove in the rounded edge for my knees to rest in and, leaning over, began to cut a narrow foothold on the steep, smooth side. When I was doing this, Stickeen came up behind me, pushed his head over my shoulder, looked into the crevasses and along the narrow knife-edge, then turned and looked in my face, muttering and whining as if trying to say, "Surely you are not going down there." I said, "Yes, Stickeen, this is the only way." He then began to cry and ran wildly along the rim of the crevasse, searching for a better way, then, returning baffled, of course, he came behind me and lay down and cried louder and louder.

After getting down one step I cautiously stooped and cut another and another in succession until I reached the point where the sliver was attached to the wall. There, cautiously balancing, I chipped down the upcurved end of the bridge until I had formed a small level platform about a foot wide, then, bending forward, got astride of the end of the sliver, steadied myself with my knees, then cut off the top of the sliver, hitching myself forward an inch or two at a time, leaving it about four inches wide for Stickeen. Arrived at the farther end of the sliver, which was about seventy-five feet long, I chipped another little platform on its upcurved end, cautiously rose to my feet, and with infinite pains cut narrow notch steps and finger-holds in the wall and finally got safely across. All this dreadful time poor little Stickeen was crying as if his heart was broken, and when I called to him in as reassuring a voice as I could muster, he only cried the louder, as if trying to say that he never, never could get down there—the only time that the brave little fellow appeared to know what danger was.

After going away as if I was leaving him, he still howled and cried without venturing to try to follow me. Returning to the edge of the crevasse, I told him that I must go, that he could come if he only tried, and finally in despair he hushed his cries, slid his little feet slowly down into my footsteps out on the big sliver, walked slowly and cautiously along the sliver as if holding his breath, while the snow was falling and the wind was moaning and threatening to blow him off. When he arrived at the foot of the slope below me, I was kneeling on the brink ready to assist him in case he should be unable to reach the top. He looked up along the row of notched steps I had made, as if fixing them in his mind, then with a nervous spring he whizzed up and passed me out on to the level ice, and ran and cried and barked and rolled about fairly hysterical in the sudden revulsion from the depth of despair to triumphant joy. I tried to catch him and pet him and tell him how good and brave he was, but he would not be caught. He ran round and round, swirling like autumn leaves in an eddy, lay down and rolled head over heels. I told him we still had far to go and that we must now stop all nonsense and get off the ice before dark. I knew by the ice-lines that every step was now taking me nearer the shore and soon it came in sight. The headland four or five miles back from the front, covered with spruce trees, loomed faintly but surely through the mist and light fall of snow not more than two miles away. The ice now proved good all the way across, and we reached the lateral moraine just at dusk, then with trembling limbs, now that the danger was over, we staggered and stumbled down the bouldery edge of the glacier and got over the dangerous rocks by the cascades while yet a faint light lingered. We were safe, and then, too, came limp weariness such as no ordinary work ever produces, however hard it may be. Wearily we stumbled down through the woods, over logs and brush and roots, devil's clubs pricking us at every faint blundering tumble. At last we got out on the smooth mud slope with only a mile of slow but sure dragging of weary limbs to camp. The Indians had been firing guns to guide me and had a fine supper and fire ready, though fearing they would be compelled to seek us in the morning, a care not often applied to me. Stickeen and I were too tired to eat much, and, strange to say, too tired to sleep. Both of us, springing up in the night again and again, fancied we were still on that dreadful ice bridge in the shadow of death.

Nevertheless, we arose next morning in newness of life. Never before had rocks and ice and trees seemed so beautiful and wonderful, even the cold, biting rainstorm that was blowing seemed full of loving-kindness, wonderful compensation for all that we had endured, and we sailed down the bay through the gray, driving rain rejoicing.

Excerpted from *Travels in Alaska*. Boston and New York: Houghton Mifflin Company, 1915.

NOTE

S. Hall Young relates in Alaska Days with John Muir *that:*

"although he was gone about seventeen hours on this day of his adventure with Stickeen, with only a bite of bread to eat, and never rested a minute of that time, but was battling with the storm all day and often racing at full speed across the glacier, yet he got up at daylight the next morning, breakfasted with me and was gone all day again, climbing a high mountain to get a view of the snow fountains and upper reaches of the glacier; and when he returned after nightfall he worked for two or three hours at his notes and sketches."

A Sled Trip on the Muir Glacier

In 1890, at 52 years of age, John Muir had spent most of the previous decade raising a family and establishing a fruit farm in Martinez, California. Having raised enough money to make his family comfortable, he returned to writing, producing, notably, a series of articles promoting the creation of Yosemite National Park. Most of his writing career still lay in front of him, and all of his future works were to be drawn from the journals he had kept of his astonishing travels. Muir had discovered Glacier Bay in 1880, but had been driven off by bad weather before he had had the opportunity to explore what was later to be known as Muir Glacier.

I STARTED OFF THE MORNING OF JULY 11 on my memorable sled-trip to obtain general views of the main upper part of the Muir Glacier and its seven principal tributaries, feeling sure that I would learn something and at the same time get rid of a severe bronchial cough that followed an attack of the grippe and had troubled me for three months. I intended to camp on the glacier every night, and did so, and my throat grew better every day until it was well, for no lowland microbe could stand such a trip. My sled was about three feet long and made as light as possible. A sack of hardtack, a little tea and sugar, and a sleeping-bag were firmly lashed on it so that nothing could drop off however much it might be jarred and dangled in crossing crevasses.

Two Indians carried the baggage over the rocky moraine to the clear glacier at the side of one of the eastern Nunatak Islands. Mr. Loomis accompanied me to this first camp and assisted in dragging the empty sled over the moraine. We arrived at the middle Nunatak Island about nine o'clock. Here I sent back my Indian carriers, and Mr. Loomis assisted me the first day in hauling the loaded sled to my second camp at the foot of Hemlock Mountain, returning the next morning.

July 13.

I skirted the mountain to eastward a few miles and was delighted to discover a group of trees high up on its ragged rocky side, the first trees I had seen on the shores of Glacier Bay or on those of any of its glaciers. I left my sled on the ice and climbed the mountain to see what I might learn. I found that all the trees were mountain hemlock (*Tsuga mertensiana*), and were evidently the remnant of an old well-established forest, standing on the only ground that was stable, all the rest of the forest below it having been sloughed off with the soil from the disintegrating slate bed rock. The lowest of the trees stood at an elevation of about two thousand feet above the sea, the highest at about three thousand feet or a little higher. Nothing could be more striking than the contrast between the raw, crumbling, deforested portions of the mountain, looking like a quarry that was being worked, and the forested part with its rich, shaggy beds of cassiope and bryanthus in full bloom, and its sumptuous cushions of flower-enameled mosses. These garden-patches are full of gay colors of gentian, erigeron, anemone, larkspur, and columbine, and are enlivened with happy birds and bees and marmots. Climbing to an elevation of twenty-five hundred feet, which is about fifteen hundred feet above the level of the glacier at this point, I saw and heard a few marmots, and three ptarmigans that were as tame as barnyard fowls. The sod is sloughing off on the edges, keeping it ragged. The trees are storm-bent from the southeast. A few are standing at an elevation of nearly three thousand feet; at twenty-five hundred feet, pyrola, veratrum, vaccinium, fine grasses, sedges, willows, mountain-ash, buttercups, and acres of the most luxuriant cassiope are in bloom.

A lake encumbered with icebergs lies at the end of Divide Glacier. A spacious, level-floored valley beyond it, eight or ten miles long, with forested mountains on its westside, perhaps discharges to the southeastward into Lynn Canal. The divide of the glacier is about opposite the third of the eastern tributaries. Another berg-dotted lake into which the drainage of the Braided Glacier flows, lies a few miles to the westward and is one and a half miles long. Berg Lake is next to the remarkable Girdled Glacier to the southeastward.

When the ice-period was in its prime, much of the Muir Glacier that now flows northward into Howling Valley flowed southward into Glacier Bay as a tributary of the Muir. All the rock contours show this, and so do the medial moraines. Berg Lake is crowded with bergs because they have no outlet and melt slowly. I heard none discharged. I had a hard time crossing the Divide Glacier, on which I camped. Half a mile back from the lake I gleaned a little fossil wood and made a fire on moraine boulders for tea. I slept fairly well on the sled. I heard the roar of four cascades on a shaggy green mountain on the west side of Howling Valley and saw three wild goats fifteen hundred feet up in the steep grassy pastures.

July 14.

I rose at four o'clock this cloudy and dismal morning and looked for my goats, but saw only one. I thought there must be wolves where there were goats, and in a few minutes heard their low, dismal, far-reaching howling. One of them sounded very near and came nearer until it seemed to be less than a quarter of a mile away on the edge of the glacier. They had evidently seen me, and one or more had come down to observe me, but I was unable to catch sight of any of them. About half an hour later, while I was eating breakfast, they began howling again, so near I began to fear they had a mind to attack me, and I made haste to the shelter of a big square boulder, where, though I had no gun, I might be able to defend myself from a front attack with my alpenstock. After waiting half an hour or so to see what these wild dogs meant to do, I ventured to proceed on my journey to the foot of Snow Dome, where I camped for the night.

There are six tributaries on the northwest side of Divide arm, counting to the Gray Glacier, next after Granite Cañon Glacier going northwest. Next is Dirt Glacier, which is dead. I saw bergs on the edge of the main glacier a mile back from here which seem to have been left by the draining of a pool in a sunken hollow. A circling rim of driftwood, back twenty rods on the glacier, marks the edge of the lakelet shore where the bergs lie scattered and stranded. It is now half past ten o'clock and getting dusk as I sit by my little fossil-wood fire writing these notes. A strange bird is calling and complaining. A stream is rushing into a glacier well on the edge of which I am camped, back a few yards from the base of the mountain for fear of falling stones. A few small ones are rattling down the steep slope. I must go to bed.

July 15.

I climbed the dome to plan a way, scan the glacier, and take bearings, etc., in case of storms. The main divide is about fifteen hundred feet; the second divide, about fifteen hundred also, is about one and one half miles southeastward. The flow of water on the glacier noticeably diminished last night though there was no frost. It is now already increasing. Stones begin to roll into the crevasses and into new positions, sliding against each other, half turning over or falling on moraine ridges. Mud pellets with small pebbles slip and roll slowly from ice-hummocks again and again. How often and by how many ways are boulders finished and finally brought to anything like permanent form and place in beds for farms and fields, forests and gardens. Into crevasses and out again, into moraines, shifted and reinforced and reformed by avalanches, melting from pedestals, etc. Rain, frost, and dew help in the work; they are swept in rills, caught and ground in pot-hole mills. Moraines of washed pebbles, like those on glacier margins, are formed by slow avalanches deposited in crevasses, then weathered out and projected on the ice as shallow raised moraines. There is one such at this camp.

A ptarmigan is on a rock twenty yards distant, as if on show. It has red over the eye, a white line, not conspicuous, over the red, belly white, white markings over the upper parts on ground of brown and black wings, mostly white as seen when flying, but the coverts the same as the rest of the body. Only about three inches of the folded primaries show white. The breast seems to have golden iridescent colors, white under the wings. It allowed me to approach within twenty feet. It walked down a sixty degree slope of the rock, took flight with a few whirring wingbeats, then sailed with wings perfectly motionless four hundred yards down a gentle grade, and vanished over the brow of a cliff. Ten days ago Loomis told me that he found a nest with nine eggs. On the way down to my sled I saw four more ptarmigans. They utter harsh notes when alarmed. "Crack, chuck, crack," with the *r* rolled and prolonged. I also saw fresh and old goat-tracks and some bones that suggest wolves.

There is a pass through the mountains at the head of the third glacier. Fine mountains stand at the head on each side. The one on the northeast side is the higher and finer every way. It has three glaciers, tributary to the third. The third glacier has altogether ten tributaries, five on each side. The mountain on the left side of White Glacier is about six thousand feet high. The moraines of Girdled Glacier seem scarce to run anywhere. Only a little material is carried to Berg Lake. Most of it seems to be at rest as a terminal on the main glacier-field, which here has little motion. The curves of these last as seen from this mountain-top are very beautiful.

It has been a glorious day, all pure sunshine. An hour or more before sunset the distant mountains, a vast host, seemed more softly ethereal than ever, pale blue, ineffably fine, all angles and harshness melted off in the soft evening light. Even the snow and the grinding, cascading glaciers became divinely tender and fine in this celestial amethystine light. I got back to camp at 7:15, not tired. After my hardtack supper I could have climbed the mountain again and got back before sunrise, but dragging the sled tires me. I have been out on the glacier examining a moraine-like mass about a third of a mile from camp. It is perhaps a mile long, a hundred yards wide, and is thickly strewn with wood. I think that it has been brought down the mountain by a heavy snow avalanche, loaded on the ice, then carried away from the shore in the direction of the flow of the glacier. This explains detached moraine-masses. This one seems to have been derived from a big roomy cirque or amphitheatre on the northwest side of this Snow Dome Mountain.

To shorten the return journey I was tempted to glissade down what appeared to be a snow-filled ravine, which was very steep. All went well until I reached a bluish spot which proved to be ice, on which I lost control of myself and rolled into a gravel talus at the foot without a scratch. Just as I got up and was getting myself orientated, I heard a loud fierce scream, uttered in an exulting, diabolical tone of voice which startled me, as if an enemy, having seen me fall, was glorying in my death. Then suddenly two ravens came swooping from the sky and alighted on the jag of a rock within a few feet of me, evidently hoping that I had been maimed and that they were going to have a feast. But as they stared at me, studying my condition, impatiently waiting for bone-picking time, I saw what they were up to and shouted, "Not yet, not yet!"

July 16.

At 7 A.M. I left camp to cross the main glacier. Six ravens came to the camp as soon as I left. What wonderful eyes they must have! Nothing that moves in all this icy wilderness escapes the eyes of these brave birds. This is one of the loveliest mornings I ever saw in Alaska; not a cloud or faintest hint of one in all the wide sky. There is a yellowish haze in the east, white in the west, mild and mellow as a Wisconsin Indian Summer, but finer, more ethereal, God's holy light making all divine.

In an hour or so I came to the confluence of the first of the seven grand tributaries of the main Muir Glacier and had a glorious view of it as it comes sweeping down in wild cascades from its magnificent, pure white, mountain-girt basin to join the main crystal sea, its many fountain peaks, clustered and crowded, all pouring forth their tribute to swell its grand current. I crossed its front a little below its confluence, where its shattered current, about two or three miles wide, is reunited, and many rills and good-sized brooks glide gurgling and ringing in pure blue channels, giving delightful animation to the icy solitude.

Most of the ice-surface crossed to-day has been very uneven, and hauling the sled and finding a way over hummocks has been fatiguing. At times I had to lift the sled bodily and to cross many narrow, nerve-trying, ice-sliver bridges, balancing astride of them, and cautiously shoving the sled ahead of me with tremendous chasms on either side. I had made perhaps not more than six or eight miles in a straight line by six o'clock this evening when I reached ice so hummocky and tedious I concluded to camp and not try to take the sled any farther. I intend to leave it here in the middle of the basin and carry my sleeping-bag and provisions the rest of the way across to the west side. I am cozy and comfortable here resting in the midst of glorious icy scenery, though very tired. I made out to get a cup of tea by means of a few shavings and splinters whittled from the bottom board of my sled, and made a fire in a little can, a small campfire, the smallest I ever made or saw, yet it answered well enough as far as tea was concerned. I crept into my sack before eight o'clock as the wind was cold and my feet wet. One of my shoes is about worn out. I may have to put on a wooden sole. This day has been cloudless throughout, with lovely sunshine, a purple evening and morning. The circumference of mountains beheld from the midst of this world of ice is marvelous, the vast plain reposing in such soft tender light, the fountain mountains so clearly cut, holding themselves aloft with their loads of ice in supreme strength and beauty of architecture. I found a skull and most of the other bones of a goat on the glacier about two miles from the nearest land. It had probably been chased out of its mountain home by wolves and devoured here. I carried its horns with me. I saw many considerable depressions in the glacial surface, also a pitlike hole, irregular, not like the ordinary wells along the slope of the many small dirt-clad hillocks, faced to the south. Now the sun is down and the sky is saffron yellow, blending and fading into purple around to the south and north. It is a curious experience to be lying in bed writing these notes, hummock waves rising in every direction, their edges marking a multitude of crevasses and pits, while all around the horizon rise peaks innumerable of most intricate style of architecture. Solemnly growling and grinding moulins contrast with the sweet low-voiced whispering and warbling of a network of rills, singing like water-ouzels, glinting, gliding with indescribable softness and sweetness of voice. They are all around, one within a few feet of my hard sled bed.

July 17.

Another glorious cloudless day is dawning in yellow and purple and soon the sun over the eastern peak will blot out the blue peak shadows and make all the vast white ice prairie sparkle. I slept well last night in the middle of the icy sea. The wind was cold but my sleeping-bag enabled me to lie neither warm nor intolerably cold. My three months' cough is gone. Strange that with such work and exposure one should know nothing of sore throats and of what are called colds. My heavy, thick-soled shoes, resoled just before starting on the trip six days ago, are about worn out and my feet have been wet every night. But no harm comes of it, nothing but good. I succeeded in getting a warm breakfast in bed. I reached over the edge of my sled, got hold of a small cedar stick that I had been carrying, whittled a lot of thin shavings from it, stored them on my breast, then set fire to a piece of paper in a shallow tin can, added a pinch of shavings, held the cup of water that always stood at my bedside over the tiny blaze with one hand, and fed the fire by adding little pinches of shavings until the water boiled, then pulling my bread sack within reach, made a good warm breakfast, cooked and eaten in bed. Thus refreshed, I surveyed the wilderness of crevassed, hummocky ice and concluded to try to drag my little sled a mile or two farther, then, finding encouragement, persevered, getting it across innumerable crevasses and streams and around several lakes and over and through the midst of hummocks, and at length reached the western shore between five and six o'clock this evening, extremely fatigued. This I consider a hard job well done, crossing so wildly broken a glacier, fifteen miles of it from Snow Dome Mountain, in two days with a sled weighing altogether not less than a hundred pounds. I found innumerable crevasses, some of them brimful of water. I crossed in most places just where the ice was close pressed and welded after descending cascades and was being shoved over an upward slope, thus closing the crevasses at the bottom, leaving only the upper sun-melted beveled portion open for water to collect in.

Vast must be the drainage from this great basin. The waste in sunshine must be enormous, while in dark weather rains and winds also melt the ice and add to the volume produced by the rain itself. The winds also, though in temperature they may be only a degree or two above freezing-point, dissolve the ice as fast, or perhaps faster, than clear sunshine. Much of the water caught in tight crevasses doubtless freezes during the winter and gives rise to many of the irregular veins seen in the structure of the glacier. Saturated snow also freezes at times and is incorporated with the ice, as only from the lower part of the glacier is the snow melted during the summer. I have noticed many traces of this action. One of the most beautiful things to be seen on the glacier is the myriads of minute and intensely brilliant radiant lights burning in rows on the banks of streams and pools and lakelets from the tips of crystals melting in the sun, making them look as if bordered with diamonds. These gems are rayed like stars and twinkle; no diamond radiates keener or more brilliant light. It was perfectly glorious to think of this divine light burning over all this vast crystal sea in such ineffably fine effulgence, and over how many other of icy Alaska's glaciers where nobody sees it. To produce these effects I fancy the ice must be melting rapidly, as it was being melted to-day. The ice in these pools does not melt with anything like an even surface, but in long branches and leaves, making fairy forests of points, while minute bubbles of air are constantly being set free. I am camped to-night on what I call Quarry Mountain from its raw, loose, plantless condition, seven or eight miles above the front of the glacier. I found enough fossil wood for tea. Glorious is the view to the eastward from this camp. The sun has set, a few clouds appear, and a torrent rushing down a gully and under the edge of the glacier is making a solemn roaring. No tinkling, whistling rills this night. Ever and anon I hear a falling boulder. I have had a glorious and instructive day, but am excessively weary and to bed I go.

July 18.

I felt tired this morning and meant to rest to-day. But after breakfast at 8 A.M. I felt I must be up and doing, climbing, sketching new views up the great tributaries from the top of Quarry Mountain. Weariness vanished and I could have climbed I think, five thousand feet. Anything seems easy after sled-dragging over hummocks and crevasses, and the constant nerve-strain in jumping crevasses so as not to slip in making the spring. Quarry Mountain is the barest I have seen, a raw quarry with infinite abundance of loose decaying granite all on the go. Its slopes are excessively steep. A few patches of epilobium make gay purple spots of color. Its seeds fly everywhere seeking homes. Quarry Mountain is cut across into a series of parallel ridges by oversweeping ice. It is still overswept in three places by glacial flows a half to three quarters of a mile wide, finely arched at the top of the divides. I have been sketching, though my eyes are much inflamed and I can scarce see. All the lines I make appear double. I fear I shall not be able to make the few more sketches I want to-morrow, but must try. The day has been gloriously sunful, the glacier pale yellow toward five o'clock. The hazy air, white with a yellow tinge, gives an Indian-summer-ish effect. Now the blue evening shadows are creeping out over the icy plain, some ten miles long, with sunny yellow belts between them. Boulders fall now and again with dull, blunt booming, and the gravel pebbles rattle.

July 19.

Nearly blind. The light is intolerable and I fear I may be long unfitted for work. I have been lying on my back all day with a snow poultice bound over my eyes. Every object I try to look at seems double; even the distant mountain-ranges are doubled, the upper an exact copy of the lower, though somewhat faint. This is the first time in Alaska that I have had too much sunshine. About four o'clock this afternoon, when I was waiting for the evening shadows to enable me to get nearer the main camp, where I could be more easily found in case my eyes should become still more inflamed and I should be unable to travel, thin clouds cast a grateful shade over all the glowing landscape. I gladly took advantage of these kindly clouds to make an effort to cross the few miles of the glacier that lay between me and the shore of the inlet. I made a pair of goggles but am afraid to wear them. Fortunately the ice here is but little broken, therefore I pulled my cap well down and set off about five o'clock. I got on pretty well and camped on the glacier in sight of the main camp, which from here in a straight line is only five or six miles away. I went ashore on Granite Island and gleaned a little fossil wood with which I made tea on the ice.

July 20.

I kept wet bandages on my eyes last night as long as I could, and feel better this morning, but all the mountains still seem to have double summits, giving a curiously unreal aspect to the landscape. I packed everything on the sled and moved three miles farther down the glacier, where I want to make measurements. Twice today I was visited on the ice by a hummingbird, attracted by the red lining of the bearskin sleeping-bag.

I have gained some light on the formation of gravel-beds along the inlet. The material is mostly sifted and sorted by successive rollings and washings along the margins of the glacier-tributaries, where the supply is abundant beyond anything I ever saw elsewhere. The lowering of the surface of a glacier when its walls are not too steep leaves a part of the margin dead and buried and protected from the wasting sunshine beneath the lateral moraines. Thus a marginal valley is formed, clear ice on one side, or nearly so, buried ice on the other. As melting goes on, the marginal trough, or valley, grows deeper and wider, since both sides are being melted, the land side slower. The dead, protected ice in melting first sheds off the large boulders, as they are not able to lie on slopes where smaller ones can. Then the next larger ones are rolled off, and pebbles and sand in succession. Meanwhile this material is subjected to torrent-action, as if it were cast into a trough. When floods come it is carried forward and stratified, according to the force of the current, sand, mud, or larger material. This exposes fresh surfaces of ice and melting goes on again, until enough material has been undermined to form a veil in front; then follows another washing and carrying-away and depositing where the current is allowed to spread. In melting, protected margin terraces are oftentimes formed. Perhaps these terraces mark successive heights of the glacial surface. From terrace to terrace the grist of stone is rolled and sifted. Some, meeting only feeble streams, have only the fine particles carried away and deposited in smooth beds: others, coarser, from swifter streams, overspread the fine beds, while many of the large boulders no doubt roll back upon the glacier to go on their travels again.

It has been cloudy mostly to-day, though sunny in the afternoon, and my eyes are getting better. The steamer Queen is expected in a day or two, so I must try to get down to the inlet tomorrow and make signal to have some of the Reid party ferry me over. I must hear from home, write letters, get rest and more to eat.

Near the front of the glacier the ice was perfectly free, apparently, of anything like a crevasse, and in walking almost carelessly down it I stopped opposite the large granite Nunatak Island, thinking that I would there be partly sheltered from the wind. I had not gone a dozen steps toward the island when I suddenly dropped into a concealed water-filled crevasse, which on the surface showed not the slightest sign of its existence. This crevasse like many others was being used as the channel of a stream, and at some narrow point the small cubical masses of ice into which the glacier surface disintegrates were jammed and extended back farther and farther till they completely covered and concealed the water. Into this I suddenly plunged, after crossing thousands of really dangerous crevasses, but never before had I encountered a danger so completely concealed. Down I plunged over head and ears, but of course bobbed up again, and after a hard struggle succeeded in dragging myself out over the farther side. Then I pulled my sled over close to Nunatak cliff, made haste to strip off my clothing, threw it in a sloppy heap and crept into my sleeping-bag to shiver away the night as best I could.

July 21.

Dressing this rainy morning was a miserable job, but might have been worse. After wringing my sloppy underclothing, getting it on was far from pleasant. My eyes are better and I feel no bad effect from my icy bath. The last trace of my three months' cough is gone. No lowland grippe microbe could survive such experiences.

I have had a fine telling day examining the ruins of the old forest of Sitka spruce that no great time ago grew in a shallow mud-filled basin near the southwest corner of the glacier. The trees were protected by a spur of the mountain that puts out here, and when the glacier advanced they were simply flooded with fine sand and overborne. Stumps by the hundred, three to fifteen feet high, rooted in a stream of fine blue mud on cobbles, still have their bark on. A stratum of decomposed bark, leaves, cones, and old trunks is still in place. Some of the stumps are on rocky ridges of gravelly soil about one hundred and twenty-five feet above the sea. The valley has been washed out by the stream now occupying it, one of the glacier's draining streams a mile longer more and an eighth of a mile wide.

I got supper early and was just going to bed, when I was startled by seeing a man coming across the moraine, Professor Reid, who had seen me from the main camp and who came with Mr. Loomis and the cook in their boat to ferry me over. I had not intended making signals for them until to-morrow but was glad to go. I had been seen also by Mr. Case and one of his companions, who were on the western mountain-side above the fossil forest, shooting ptarmigans. I had a good rest and sleep and leisure to find out how rich I was in new facts and pictures and how tired and hungry I was.

Excerpted from *Travels in Alaska*. Boston and New York: Houghton Mifflin Company, 1915.

Nearly Crushed by an Iceberg

John Muir survived the following adventure and lived for another twenty years. While he engaged in no more documented life-endangering activities, he stayed active and healthy. Within a month of his escape from the iceberg, he returned home to see Yosemite, Sequoia and General Grant National Parks become a reality. In 1892, he founded the Sierra Club with several others from the San Francisco Bay area, and became its first president, a position he held until his death. He wrote passionately for wilderness preservation, over the course of his life publishing ten books and three hundred articles. He escorted Presidents Roosevelt and Taft to Yosemite. He travelled around the world twice, chasing down rumors of trees larger than his beloved sequoia, delighted that he never found one. He discovered and explored the Black Forest in Arizona.

Muir passed quietly away of pneumonia on Christmas Eve, 1914, in Los Angeles. Pages from the unfinished manuscript of Travels in Alaska, *the source of this excerpt, lay strewn about his bedside.*

A FEW DAYS LATER I SET OUT with Professor Reid's party to visit some of the other large glaciers that flow into the bay, to observe what changes have taken place in them since October, 1879, when I first visited and sketched them. We found the upper half of the bay closely choked with bergs, through which it was exceedingly difficult to force a way. After slowly struggling a few miles up the east side, we dragged the whale-boat and canoe over rough rocks into a fine garden and comfortably camped for the night.

The next day was spent in cautiously picking a way across to the west side of the bay; and as the strangely scanty stock of provisions was already about done, and the ice-jam to the northward seemed impenetrable, the party decided to return to the main camp by a comparatively open, roundabout way to the southward, while with the canoe and a handful of food-scraps I pushed on northward. After a hard, anxious struggle, I reached the mouth of the Hugh Miller fiord about sundown, and tried to find a campspot on its steep, boulder-bound shore. But no landing-place where it seemed possible to drag the canoe above high-tide mark was discovered after examining a mile or more of this dreary, forbidding barrier, and as night was closing down, I decided to try to grope my way across the mouth of the fiord in the starlight to an open sandy spot on which I had camped in October, 1879, a distance of about three or four miles.

With the utmost caution I picked my way through the sparkling bergs, and after an hour or two of this nerve-trying work, when I was perhaps less than halfway across and dreading the loss of the frail canoe which would include the loss of myself, I came to a pack of very large bergs which loomed threateningly, offering no visible thoroughfare. Paddling and pushing to right and left, I at last discovered a sheer-walled opening about four feet wide and perhaps two hundred feet long, formed apparently by the splitting of a huge iceberg. I hesitated to enter this passage, fearing that the slightest change in the tide-current might close it, but ventured nevertheless, judging that the dangers ahead might not be greater than those I had already passed. When I had got about a third of the way in, I suddenly discovered that the smooth-walled ice-lane was growing narrower, and with desperate haste backed out. Just as the bow of the canoe cleared the sheer walls they came together with a growling crunch. Terror-stricken, I turned back, and in an anxious hour or two gladly reached the rock-bound shore that had at first repelled me, determined to stay on guard all night in the canoe or find some place where with the strength that comes in a fight for life I could drag it up the boulder wall beyond ice danger. This at last was happily done about midnight, and with no thought of sleep I went to bed rejoicing.

My bed was two boulders, and as I lay wedged and bent on their upbulging sides, beguiling the hard, cold time in gazing into the starry sky and across the sparkling bay, magnificent upright bars of light in bright prismatic colors suddenly appeared, marching swiftly in close succession along the northern horizon from west to east as if in diligent haste, an auroral display very different from any I had ever before beheld. Once long ago in Wisconsin I saw the heavens draped in rich purple auroral clouds fringed and folded in most magnificent forms; but in this glory of light, so pure, so bright, so enthusiastic in motion, there was nothing in the least cloudlike. The short color-bars, apparently about two degrees in height, through blending, seemed to be as well defined as those of the solar spectrum.

How long these glad, eager soldiers of light held on their way I cannot tell; for sense of time was charmed out of mind and the blessed night circled away in measureless rejoicing enthusiasm.

In the early morning after so inspiring a night I launched my canoe feeling able for anything, crossed the mouth of the Hugh Miller fiord, and forced a way three or four miles along the shore of the bay, hoping to reach the Grand Pacific Glacier in front of Mt. Fairweather. But the farther I went, the ice-pack, instead of showing inviting little open streaks here and there, became so much harder jammed that on some parts of the shore the bergs, drifting south with the tide, were shoving one another out of the water beyond high-tide line. Farther progress to northward was thus rigidly stopped, and now I had to fight for a way back to my cabin, hoping that by good tide luck I might reach it before dark. But at sundown I was less than half-way home, and though very hungry was glad to land on a little rock island with a smooth beach for the canoe and a ticket of alder bushes for fire and bed and a little sleep. But shortly after sundown, while these arrangements were being made, lo and behold another aurora enriching the heavens! and though it proved to be one of the ordinary almost colorless kind, thrusting long, quivering lances toward the zenith from a dark cloudlike base, after last night's wonderful display one's expectations might well be extravagant and I lay wide awake watching.

On the third night I reached my cabin and food. Professor Reid and his party came in to talk over the results of our excursions, and just as the last one of the visitors opened the door after bidding good-night, he shouted, "Muir, come look here. Here's something fine."

I ran out in auroral excitement, and sure enough here was another aurora, as novel and wonderful as the marching rainbow-colored columns—a glowing silver bow spanning the Muir Inlet in a magnificent arch right under the zenith, or a little to the south of it, the ends resting on the top of the mountain-walls. And though colorless and steadfast, its intense, solid, white splendor, noble proportions, and fineness of finish excited boundless admiration. In form and proportion it was like a rainbow, a bridge of one span five miles wide; and so brilliant, so fine and solid and homogeneous in every part, I fancy that if all the stars were raked together into one window, fused and welded and run through some celestial rolling-mill, all would be required to make this one glowing white colossal bridge.

After my last visitor went to bed, I lay down on the moraine in front of the cabin and gazed and watched. Hour after hour the wonderful arch stood perfectly motionless, sharply defined and substantial-looking as if it were a permanent addition to the furniture of the sky. At length while it yet spanned the inlet in serene unchanging splendor, a band of fluffy, pale gray, quivering ringlets came suddenly all in a row over the eastern mountain-top, glided in nervous haste up and down the under side of the bow and over the western mountain-wall. They were about one and a half times the apparent diameter of the bow in length, maintained a vertical posture all the way across, and slipped swiftly along as if they were suspended like a curtain on rings. Had these lively auroral fairies marched across the fiord on the top of the bow instead of shuffling along the under side of it, one might have fancied they were a happy band of spirit people on a journey making use of the splendid bow for a bridge. There must have been hundreds of miles of them; for the time required for each to cross from one end of the bridge to the other seemed only a minute or less, while nearly an hour elapsed from their first appearance until the last of the rushing throng vanished behind the western mountain, leaving the bridge as bright and solid and steadfast as before they arrived. But later, half an hour or so, it began to fade. Fissures or cracks crossed it diagonally through which a few stars were seen, and gradually it became thin and nebulous until it looked like the Milky Way, and at last vanished, leaving no visible monument of any sort to mark its place.

I now returned to my cabin, replenished the fire, warmed myself, and prepared to go to bed, though too aurorally rich and happy to go to sleep. But just as I was about to retire, I thought I had better take another look at the sky, to make sure that the glorious show was over; and, contrary to all reasonable expectations, I found that the pale foundation for another bow was being laid right overhead like the first. Then losing all thought of sleep, I ran back to my cabin, carried out blankets and lay down on the moraine to keep watch until daybreak, that none of the sky wonders of the glorious night within reach of my eyes might be lost.

I had seen the first bow when it stood complete in full splendor, and its gradual fading decay. Now I was to see the building of a new one from the beginning. Perhaps in less than half an hour the silvery material was gathered, condensed, and welded into a glowing, evenly proportioned arc like the first and in the same part of the sky. Then in due time over the eastern mountain-wall came another throng of restless electric auroral fairies, the infinitely fine pale-gray garments of each lightly touching those of their neighbors as they swept swiftly along the under side of the bridge and down over the western mountain like the merry band that had gone the same way before them, all keeping quivery step and time to music too fine for mortal ears.

While the gay throng was gliding swiftly along, I watched the bridge for any change they might make upon it, but not the slightest could I detect. They left no visible track, and after all had passed the glowing arc stood firm and apparently immutable, but at last faded slowly away like its glorious predecessor.

Excepting only the vast purple aurora mentioned above, said to have been visible over nearly all the continent, these two silver bows in supreme, serene, supernal beauty surpassed everything auroral I ever beheld.

Excerpted from *Travels in Alaska*. Boston and New York: Houghton Mifflin Company, 1915.

Milestones in the Life of John Muir

1838 Born in Dunbar, Scotland, April 21.

1849 Emigrated with family to Wisconsin frontier.

1860 Won prize for inventions at State Agricultural Fair.
Entered University of Wisconsin.

1864–1866 Botanized in Canada.

1867 Walked from Kentucky to Florida.
Wrote first jounal.

1868 Arrived in California, March 28.

1868–1873 Made Yosemite Valley his headquarters.
Explored Sierra for evidence of glacial action.

1874–1876 Climbed Mount Shasta.
Began intensive study of trees.
Launched movement for federal control of forests.

1879 First trip to Alaska.

1880 Married Louie Wanda Strentzel, April.
Second trip to Alaska.

1881 Cruised in Alaskan and Arctic waters.

1882–1887 Home and fruit-raising.

1888 Ascended Mount Rainier.
Resumed writing.

1889 Worked for the creation of Yosemite National Park.

1890 Yosemite National Park Bill passed by Congress.
Explored Muir Glacier in Alaska.

1891–1892	Founded Sierra Club.
	Worked for recession of Yosemite Valley and the Mariposa Grove of Giant Sequoias to federal government.
1893–1894	Visited Europe.
	Mountains of California published.
1896–1898	Received M.A. from Harvard,
	LL.D. from University of Wisconsin.
1899	Joined the Harriman-Alaska expedition.
1901-1902	*Our National Parks* published.
	Began fight to save Hetch Hetchy Valley.
1903	Guided President Theodore Roosevelt through Yosemite.
1905	Yosemite Valley receded to federal control.
	Death of Mrs. Muir, August.
1906	Explored Arizona.
1909	*Stickeen* published.
1911	*My First Summer in the Sierra* published.
	Received LITT.D. from Yale.
1913	*Story of My Boyhood and Youth* published.
	LL.D. from University of California.
	Lost fight to save Hetch Hetchy Valley.
1914	Died in Los Angeles, December 24.

ABOUT LEE STETSON

Lee Stetson is a well-known actor who has been portraying John Muir in one-person productions since 1983. He has considerable stage experience, and has written a number of plays for himself and others. Stetson had occasion to read many of Muir's books and articles in the process of developing his shows, and was struck by the fact that Muir's entertaining outdoor adventures had never been collected in one volume. Believing that these stories are examples of Muir's best and most engaging prose, Stetson conceived this book.

Stetson's theatrical presentations of his Muir characterization occur regularly every summer in Yosemite National Park, and in venues throughout the United States and the world during other times of the year. His performances incorporate the adventures included in this volume and many others. He resides with his wife Connie in El Portal, California, at Yosemite's doorstep.

ABOUT FIONA KING

Fiona King was born in Scotland, raised in Alberta, Canada, and has been a freelance illustrator for about eight years. Primarily self-taught, she has done work for many agencies and publishers throughout the United States. She resides at Lake Hodges in southern California.

BOOK DESIGN BY SANDY BELL
in Springdale, Utah

❦

Composed in Birch and Caslon typefaces.
This edition is printed on
acid-free paper that is also 50% recycled,
by McNaughton & Gunn, Inc.,
Saline, Michigan.